shed
nds,
avel.

our
rets
rld,
th of
experience and a passion for travel.

Rely on Thomas Cook as your travelling companion on your next trip and benefit from our unique heritage.

Thomas Cook **pocket** guides

BUDAPEST

Your travelling companion since 1873

Thomas Cook

Written by Carolyn Zukowski, updated by Wendy Wrangham

Published by Thomas Cook Publishing
A division of Thomas Cook Tour Operations Limited
Company registration no. 3772199 England
The Thomas Cook Business Park, Unit 9, Coningsby Road,
Peterborough PE3 8SB, United Kingdom
Email: books@thomascook.com, Tel: +44 (0) 1733 416477
www.thomascookpublishing.com

Produced by Cambridge Publishing Management Limited
Burr Elm Court, Main Street, Caldecote CB23 7NU
www.cambridgepm.co.uk

ISBN: 978-1-84848-435-1

Series Editor: Karen Beaulah
Production/DTP: Steven Collins

Printed and bound in Spain by GraphyCems

CONTENTS

SYMBOLS KEY

The following symbols are used throughout this book:

ⓐ address ☎ telephone ⓦ website address ⓔ email
🕒 opening times Ⓝ public transport connections ❶ important

The following symbols are used on the maps:

𝒾	information office	▪	point of interest
✈	airport	○	city
✚	hospital	○	large town
⊙	police station	○	small town
🚌	bus station	═	motorway
🚆	railway station	—	main road
Ⓜ	metro		minor road
✝	cathedral	—	railway
❶	numbers denote featured cafés & restaurants		

Hotels and restaurants are graded by approximate price as follows:
£ budget price ££ mid-range price £££ expensive

▶ *One of the statues atop Gellért Hill*

INTRODUCING
Budapest

Introduction

While the rest of Hungary leisurely wakes up to the 21st century, Budapest has already had three coffee breaks and is zooming light years ahead. It's a city that's eager to adopt new trends while resolutely mindful of its dark and bullet-pocked past.

The key lies in understanding its history, marked by periods of great wealth and prosperity, and by devastating eras of political and social upheaval. Repeated warfare was inevitable due to the strategic location of Budapest, spreading out on either side of the Duna (River Danube) in the heart of Europe. The location of the city is strategic in a cultural sense as well. Baulking at the idea of being lumped with the Balkans or other eastern European nations, Budapesters are proud that their 'Paris of the East' has inspired native sons Béla Bartók, László Bíró, Andy Grove and Ernő Rubik.

History braids itself with tradition while keeping its eye on the future. You will capture the unpretentious, homely feeling of Budapest while sitting on a sleek, modernised tram as it zips quietly past weathered yet wonderfully regal architecture. Ten times larger than any other Hungarian city, this confident and cosmopolitan Magyar metropolis is a major European capital with heart. The neon lights and legions of tourists will only distract you briefly from its famous crooked, cobbled streets, secret alleyways, wide boulevards, atmospheric bridges and tranquil parks.

It's a city of largesse, with the best Turkish baths, the first metro system in continental Europe, the highest-ranked European 5-star hotel, the second Michelin star in central and eastern Europe, the largest collection of Hungarian art anywhere, the second-largest synagogue in the world, the largest collection of preserved Soviet statuary outside Russia, the highest number of Jewish residents per capita of any European city and the most intact Jewish ghetto in Europe.

Mainly, it's a city of superlatives, doing its Buda*best* to keep you here longer than you intended.

Budapest is a trove of colourful medieval architecture

When to go

Budapest is a top destination at any time of year, though if you're sensitive to temperature, it's a good idea to avoid the extremes of summer and winter (see below). That aside, come whenever you like – there's no 'off' switch on Budapest's fun button.

SEASONS & CLIMATE

Budapest is fire and ice. Expect the summer to be very hot and dry, but with any luck a cool breeze will be blowing off the Danube. Autumn months are spectacular, but often chilly, and winter is downright cold, and sometimes snowy, with average temperatures between −4°C (25°F) and 4°C (39°F). Spring is the most pleasant time in the city, before the tourist season kicks off, though rain can dampen your spirits. Luckily, Budapest is a modern city offering comfortable public transport whatever the weather, and most places you will visit have air conditioning and central heating.

ANNUAL EVENTS

March–April

Spring Festival The tourist season in Budapest kicks off with this month-long celebration, featuring world-class performers of classical music, opera, literature and theatre in a variety of glittery Budapest venues. There's also a series of open-air events, including parades and markets that beckon in the spring with style. ⓦ www.festivalcity.hu

Titanic International Film Festival (last week Mar–early Apr) Dozens of screenings of internationally acclaimed art and cult films from Asia, Europe and North America at venues across the city. ⓦ www.titanicfilmfest.hu

Easter Monday (9 Apr 2012; 1 Apr 2013) This is largely an excuse to get drunk. In Budapest, men visit their girlfriends, spray them with cheap perfume and receive a stiff drink of *pálinka* (brandy) in return. The hangovers on Tuesday are brutal.

May

May Day (1 May) Once upon a time, this was a Communist holiday (Labour Day), but now it's just an excuse to go outside and listen to the open-air musical entertainment in the city's parks. Dance around the maypole or go to a rock concert on the outdoor stage in Tabán in Buda.

The Budapest Wine Festival is an annual event held at the castle

June–August

Worldwide Music Day (closest weekend to Midsummer Day – 21 June) This musical event is big throughout Hungary – every town features some kind of concert. Budapest opens its doors (and ears) to jazz, folk and rock musicians in the Városliget, Népliget and Klauzál parks.
Summer on the Chain Bridge (late June–mid-Aug) Every weekend in early summer, the arts take over the Lánchíd (Chain Bridge), which connects Buda and Pest, with a lively promenade of painters, musicians, dancers and musical groups. Ⓦ www.festivalcity.hu
Budafest Summer Music Festival (July & Aug) A highbrow musical event, where the venues are almost as stunning as the performances. Ballet, folk, opera and jazz all feature. Ⓦ www.viparts.hu
Hungarian Formula One Grand Prix (Aug: see website for dates) Book your tickets early for this event that brings the best and brightest of Formula 1 racing into town. The course is about 20 km (12 miles) from Budapest, in Mogyoród. Ⓦ www.formula1.com
Sziget Festival The city's magnificent music fest (see page 12).
St Stephen's Day (20 Aug) Hungarians celebrate their founding father by taking his preserved right hand about town in a religious procession. The climax features fireworks on top of Gellért Hill at 21.00.
Jewish Summer Festival (late Aug) A week-long celebration of Jewish culture, featuring music, dance, comedy, cabaret and visual arts. Ⓦ www.zsidonyarifestival.hu

September–October

Budapest Wine Festival Every year, Budai Vár (Buda Castle) is the venue for a highly competitive showdown of Hungarian wine producers fiercely pitching their vintages. This is probably the most fun you'll ever have at a trade fair. Ⓦ www.winefestival.hu
Budapest Autumn Festival The crème de la crème of Budapest's

yearly events, a contemporary fine-arts festival featuring elements of dance, cinema and theatre. Ⓦ www.festivalcity.hu

Budapest International Marathon The city is transformed into a treadmill as thousands of runners descend to work up a sweat through the streets of both Buda and Pest. Ⓦ www.budapestmarathon.com

December

Karácsony (Christmas) From noon on 24 December until the evening of 26 December, the whole city shuts down to celebrate Christmas. Even if you're not into carp, the traditional Christmas meal eaten on Christmas Eve, try it just this once. Presents are exchanged on Christmas Eve, after dinner.

Szilveszterest (New Year's Eve) Fireworks blast all over town, and public transport runs all night to take you to the pre-, post- and post-post-midnight parties. The next day is an opportunity for reaffirming healthy resolutions.

PUBLIC HOLIDAYS

New Year's Day 1 Jan

Anniversary of the 1848–9 Uprising against the Habsburgs 15 Mar

Easter Monday 9 Apr 2012, 1 Apr 2013

May Day 1 May

St Stephen's Day 20 Aug

Anniversary of the 1956 Revolution, and of the 1989 Declaration of the Independent Republic of Hungary 23 Oct

Christmas Eve 24 Dec (half-day)

Christmas Day 25 Dec

Second Day of Christmas 26 Dec

The Sziget Festival

Every August, Óbudai Island in the middle of the Danube is the stage for a celebration of musical decadence: the Sziget (Island) Festival. Warm weather, cool vibes and some of the best musical acts combine to make this temporarily built festival city one of the hottest spots in Central Europe.

Some 1,000 different programmes at 60 different venues on the island attract more than 400,000 visitors during the seven days, offering not only music, but a wide range of sporting and cultural activities, theatre performances, fine-art exhibitions, literary readings and film screenings.

Alternative, blues, electric dance, hard-rock, hip-hop, mainstream, jazz and world music pours out of every corner of the island, creating a real buzz. But many of the most exquisite experiences have nothing to do with the music: drinking that first beer in the heat of the noonday sun, chilling out in chairs made of tyres while sipping an iced *macchiato*, setting up your tent in the early evening shadows and watching other music lovers in various states of bliss.

The festival organisers cater to your every need. There are accommodation and information offices; ATMs and bureaux de change; banking and postal services; children's activities and babysitting; restaurants, pubs, shops and craft markets; lockers and left-luggage facilities; a chemist's; ground-keeping, hot showers and regularly pumped portable toilets – all take the rough out of roughing it. Police, firefighters and paramedics are on hand for emergencies. A multilingual information centre helps visitors to resolve any problems they might encounter during the week. You may even find yourself wandering into a 'Language First Aid' tent, where you can learn some basic Hungarian expressions to help you chat with the locals.

If you're not in the mood to groove, you can seek relief in bungee jumping, wall-climbing, football, volleyball and wide-open green spaces for tossing a frisbee.

There's a specially designed area on the island for caravans only. If you bring a car, you can park near the festival site or in a secure car park in Budapest. There are special buses, trains and ferries from Budapest to the festival grounds. The best bet, however, is to camp all week. You'll go home with a backpack full of smelly, beer-splashed, danced-out togs and a smile on your face. Go to www.sziget.hu for festival information.

The Sziget Festival is the place to be in August

History

For thousands of years, Celts, Romans, Huns, Mongols, Turks, Slovaks, Austrians, Germans and Russians have variously ransacked, razed and rebuilt Budapest many times over.

The Magyars, as Hungarians call themselves, were master equestrians from the steppes who rode and raided their way into western Europe until halted by the Germanic tribes in 955. Their loss of power forced them into a reluctant alliance with the Holy Roman Empire, and, in the year 1000, the Magyar prince Stephen was crowned and the nation of Hungary was born. This didn't sit well with tribes loyal to the older shamanic religion, so they sent the missionary Gellért down a hill in a spiked barrel, hoping to get their message across.

Hungary was invaded by the Mongols in the 13th century, and occupied by the Ottoman Turks in the 16th and 17th centuries. Buda developed into a provincial Ottoman town, Mátyás Templom (Matthias Church) was converted into a mosque and the hot springs underground were used to create Turkish baths.

In 1699 the Turks were ousted and the country became a province of the Austrian Habsburgs. Hungary blossomed economically and culturally, though a strong nationalistic undercurrent started to brew. Buda effectively became the German-speaking town of Ofen and by 1783 was the nation's administrative centre, while Pest became an important commercial centre. Soon, nationalistic feelings came to the surface and Hungary declared independence in 1849. The Habsburgs were able to quell the uprising with the help of the Russian army.

Passive resistance among the Hungarians, and a couple of disastrous military defeats for the Habsburgs, eventually led to the Compromise of 1867, creating the Dual Monarchy of Austria the empire and Hungary the kingdom. As a result, Buda, Pest and Óbuda united to form Budapest in 1873. That same year, Jews were given equal rights in the courts and Budapest underwent a renaissance. A massive Jewish immigration movement brought scholars and industrialists from neighbouring Russia and Poland. Many of the buildings in Budapest that you see today were built during this exciting time.

The 20th century was a horror show, with Hungary on the losing side during both world wars. Budapest suffered severe damages in World War II, with the retreating German army blowing up Buda Castle and every bridge on the Danube. In 1949, the Communists gained control, banning books, executing foreign spies and imprisoning the intelligentsia and church leaders. Again, an undercurrent of nationalism started to swell and resulted in an anti-Soviet uprising in Budapest, known as the 1956 Revolution. The Russians retaliated, leaving thousands dead in the streets and many buildings scarred with bullet holes. The Russians knew that the Hungarians were hard to break, so they instituted a system of consumer-oriented Communism, also known as 'goulash Communism', transforming Hungary into the most liberal, furthest-developed and richest nation in the region until the 1980s. Following the collapse of Communism, the nation became the Republic of Hungary in 1989.

In 2004, Hungary joined NATO and became a member of the EU. The riots of 2006, which were sparked by a leaked recording of the prime minister admitting to lying, constituted a blip on the country's otherwise upward trajectory. Elections in 2010 installed a centre-right mandate, Hungary's first non-coalition government, and the city of Budapest continues to be a central European hub of development and enterprise.

Lifestyle

Budapest is built on a fault line, both physically and psychologically. Everywhere you go in the city you notice the new butting impatiently against the old. The younger generations fill the streets with new cars, mobile phones and a sense of purpose, while old people stare out of their windows lost in memories of shocking events that shook their lives. Façades of buildings carry scars of bullet holes made 50 years ago, while the house across the street has been renovated.

But if you think that shopping centres, hypermarkets and corporate logos will take over Budapest, think again. What makes Budapest so special is its ability to straddle this fault line, rebuilding history while allowing the tinge of the past to remain. This explains the lingering popularity of the Turkish baths, the handiworks sold by Transylvanian peasant women, and the butcher who does a brisk business in the dingy blocks of flats on the city's outskirts. It also explains why westernised holidays are lost on the modern Hungarian, who would rather stick with the traditional celebrations of name days than embrace the concept of Halloween or Valentine's Day.

The Hungarians are a proud people who have spent time convincing the world that they are not an eastern European country, but a central European country. To that end, the improvements made to infrastructure over the last five or ten years have not only improved the city, but also the people's outlook in general. International cuisine is now a mainstay of the capital along with service with a smile, and Budapest has been awarded the second Michelin star in central and eastern Europe, after Prague. The idea of good customer service is a notion that has stuck, and, with it, a new-found confidence in consumerism.

In the summer, Budapesters and their families all head to Lake Balaton (fondly referred to by landlocked locals as 'the Hungarian sea') for rest and relaxation, so don't expect to get any official business done on a Friday after 14.00. Hungarians are reasonable capitalists, meaning they will work hard for their money but never lose sight of the important things in life – family, friends and fun, and the freedom to choose when to take time off.

Enjoying the sunshine in Heroes' Square

Culture

As soon as you arrive in Budapest, pick up the latest issue of one of the English-language newspapers, the *Budapest Sun* or the *Budapest Times*. Sit down at a café, relax with a map and plot your adventure.

As you'll see, Budapest offers an exhausting list of cultural possibilities, and, what's more, almost every ticket is affordable. You can still go to the Állami Operaház (State Opera House, see page 81), one of Europe's finest, for less than five pounds, so it makes sense to go to a performance, even if you don't particularly love opera or classical music. In the summer, churches and halls open their interiors to musical accompaniment and you'll hear exuberant strains of music along the Lánchíd (Chain Bridge) and in parks and gardens all over town.

The festivals in Budapest are the biggest cultural events of the year, showcasing the world's greatest musical, artistic and dramatic talents. The Sziget Festival (see page 12) is probably the best rock festival

BUDAPEST CARD

The *Budapest Kártya* (Budapest Card) provides unlimited travel on public transport, free entry to 60 museums, a couple of free tours and various sights, and discounts on everything from sightseeing tours to restaurant meals. Cards come in two- or three-day versions (6,300 HUF and 7,500 HUF, respectively) and include a decent pocket-sized brochure containing maps of Buda, Pest and the metro system. The Budapest Card brochure map clearly indicates museums, galleries and other establishments that accept the card.

during the European summer, featuring an eclectic electric line-up of world-renowned rockers, their lesser-known counterparts and local talent.

Many performances at the modern **Nemzeti Színház** (**Hungarian National Theatre** XI. Bajor Gizi Park 1 (1) 555 3000 www.nemzetiszinhaz.hu Tram: 2 to Millenniumi Kultura Központ) are in English. Not only is it exciting to sit in the controversially designed theatre on the Pest embankment, with a

The striking modern Hungarian National Theatre

stage that can be raised or lowered, lifts that offer a panoramic view of the city and a façade that's half-submerged in a pool near the main entrance, but it is also a thrilling thespian adventure to hear Shakespeare with a Hungarian accent.

You can purchase tickets for events in a number of ways. For opera, ballet, theatre or concert tickets in advance, you can save money by going to the individual venue box offices, as ticket agencies might not carry the entire price range of tickets. **Broadway Ticket Office** (ⓐ VI. Nagymező utca 19 ⓣ (1) 302 3841 Metro: Opera) sells tickets to most cultural events. If you're trying to organise tickets from abroad, **Ticket Express** (ⓦ www.eventim.hu) is a good online bet. Ticket Express booking offices are also in convenient locations all over town.

Budapest's museums are unique in that they're high-class, without being snob fests. You'll find trendy galleries in the streets lined with public art. Some of the best museums in town, the Magyar Nemzeti Galéria (Hungarian National Gallery, see page 69) or the Szépművészeti Múzeum (Museum of Fine Arts, see page 94), not only house some incredible collections, but also boast buildings that are works of art in themselves. Go to ⓦ www.exindex.hu for details of temporary exhibitions in galleries around town.

The best source of listings for English-language films is the *Budapest Sun*. Movies labelled '*szinkronizált*', '*m.b.*' or '*magyarul beszélő*' are dubbed into Hungarian; those labelled '*feliratos*' have Hungarian subtitles.

End the evening with a stop at a café. As you come to the bitter end, you'll remember why you came here in the first place: not just for affordable fun and flash, but for a rich cultural experience.

Night-time view across the Danube

MAKING THE MOST OF
Budapest

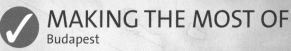

Shopping

Budapest offers an incredibly diverse array of items and places in which to purchase them. You can layer your suitcases with flea-market finds, delectable deli foodstuffs, unique folk-inspired art and designer threads. It's refreshing to find the salespeople at global fashion giants twiddling their thumbs while the peasant women on the street corner do a brisk trade in embroidered one-of-a-kind handiworks.

Hungary is famous for its flashy equestrian gear, embroideries, painted eggs, folk costumes, hand-painted porcelain, crystal, Halas lace, decorative woodcarvings and Helia-D cosmetics. Food items include red paprika, goose-liver pâté, pickled vegetables, Pick salami, or honey-soaked nuts in glass jars. If you're looking for a special bottle, buy some Tokaji (sweet white) or Egri Bikavér (dry red) wines, *pálinka* (fiery fruit brandy) or the special hangover cure, Zwack Unicum.

A shopping centre dressed in its Christmas glory

MARKETS

Budapest has some excellent *piac*, or markets, and they are great places to get a food's-eye view of the locals. Vegetarians will appreciate taking a break from the usual restaurant diet of fried mushroom and cheese dishes to find the freshest fruit, vegetables and bread. And, if you're after food on the go, try an indoor fast-food stall. For a great introduction to the region's foodstuffs, and to pack your picnic basket full, the best place to go is the Nagyvásárcsarnok (Great Market Hall, see page 98). This market is great for locally grown, fresh produce and there are stalls selling salami, bread, fruit, nuts, poppy-seed cakes and souvenirs. Or, follow the enticing smells to **Molnar's Kürtőskalács** (ⓐ V. Váci utca 31), for one of these freshly baked pastries that are a Hungarian speciality.

The markets of Budapest also offer an overwhelming assortment of antiques, folksy wares and contemporary art. Falk Miksa utca, near Margit híd (Margaret Bridge), is a thoroughfare featuring more than 20 shops with different personalities in unusual settings.

The best shopping excitement is to be had at the flea markets either in the Városliget (City Park) or at Ecseri (XIX. Nagykőrösi út 156). These are strictly for the strong-willed shopper who can discern between treasure and trash. You'll benefit from the Hungarian penchant for hoarding, be it coloured bottles with glass stoppers, retro formica tables, light fittings, weapons, medals, coins or Soviet and East German memorabilia. Snap it up now before eBay gets a whiff of the action.

Rummage through the antique shops for special bargains

Váci utca is the place to start. Little boutiques selling unique garments mingle with souvenir joints touting T-shirts, key rings and other forgettable items. There are also the more familiar outlets in the shape of **Zara** (Ⓐ V Kristóf tér Ⓣ (1) 327 0210) and **Marks & Spencer** (Ⓐ V. Váci utca 1–4 Ⓣ (1) 318 4606 or 267 0564). The fashion-conscious, or shoppers with children, will love the shopping complexes Westend City Center (see page 86), Mammut (see page 70) and **Mom Park** (Ⓐ XII. Alkotás út 53 Ⓣ (1) 487 5501). Not places to save money, but these air-conditioned spaces are great for beating the summer heat.

Label lovers will find garments galore on the prestigious Andrássy út, with its selection of exclusive shops. The Hungarian designer Katti Zoób (Ⓦ www.kattizoob.hu) has her own outlet near Margit híd (Margaret Bridge), while around the Oktogon area are small retro shops selling funky designs from independent labels – Retrock is one of the best. Also not to be missed is the newly pedestrianised Fő utca, which runs parallel to Váci utca on the Pest side of the river and has a wealth of independent shops, galleries and cafés.

USEFUL SHOPPING PHRASES

How much is this?
Mennyibe kerül ez?
Mehnj-njee-beh keh-rewl ehz?

Can I try this on?
Felpróbálhatom?
Fehl-proh-bahl-ho-tom?

My size is ...
Az én méretem ...
Oz ehn may-reh-tehm ...

I'll take this one, thank you
Ezt megveszem, köszönöm
Ehzt mehg-veh-sehm, kuh-suh-nuhm

Eating & drinking

Influenced by neighbouring countries Austria, Croatia, Slovakia, Slovenia, Romania, Serbia and the Czech Republic, Hungary serves up hearty dishes rich in flavour and calories. A combination of international flair and wholesome goodness inspired by the hills and plains of Hungary makes a meal fit for a Magyar.

The cost of dining in Budapest may have risen in recent years (legitimately, in the case of the most frightening price-hikes, where a Michelin star has been earnt), but at least you won't any longer blow your eating-out budget on imported wines.

Ever the traditionalists, Hungarians will reach for sauces rich in sour cream, fried goose liver and meat, including game such as boar and venison. Fish can feature on the Hungarian restaurant menu, especially carp or pike perch, often in the form of a thick spicy soup. Other traditional favourites include veal paprika stew, or roast chicken, with dumplings. Desserts, served with strong espresso, include strudels, *palacsinta* (sweet pancakes) and the legendary Gundel sponge cake soaked with rum and topped with chocolate sauce, custard, walnuts, raisins and whipped cream.

Vegetarians will struggle here, as traditional Hungarian fare is meat-heavy. Fill up on the creamy mushroom or onion soups (often served in a hollowed-out bread loaf) or the cheese-stuffed fried mushrooms.

PRICE CATEGORIES

Restaurants with the following symbols indicate the cost of a three-course meal, excluding drinks.

£ up to 4,000 HUF **££** 4,000–7,000 HUF **£££** over 7,000 HUF

More and more restaurants in Budapest offer lighter fare, to appeal to a more cosmopolitan palate. You'll find English-language menus in most Budapest restaurants, and friendly staff with some command of English. Modern restaurants aim to redesign the typically Hungarian dishes, using some of the best home-grown produce in Europe.

Wine connoisseurs are familiar with the Hungarian sweet white wine, Tokaji, made by a special process where the grapes are left on the vine to sweeten and shrivel in the sun. Then it's rated by *puttony* number, or number of baskets of grapes that go into the barrel. The greater the number, the sweeter and more expensive the wine. Strong red Egri Bikavér (Eger Bull's Blood) is internationally known and exported in the EU but it is very much an acquired taste.

Feast on traditional hearty Hungarian fare

Hungary boasts 16 wine-producing districts that make a wide range of wines, including Cabernet Sauvignon, Pinot Gris, Merlot, Riesling, Chardonnay, sparkling and rosé. It would be a shame not to try them all. One word of warning: it's considered bad taste to clink your beer or wine glasses. The occupying Austrians adopted this custom after they had executed the Hungarian generals who led the failed uprising of 1848–9.

End your meal with a warming shot of the 'digestive' Unicum. This secret blend of herbs and alcohol has been popular for generations and is considered a lifesaver by the locals. Its various uses are as a digestive, for getting drunk and for curing a killer hangover come the morning. Makes sense.

When it is time to pay, you may notice a service charge tacked on to your bill. In this case, you don't have to tip unless your service was outstanding. If that's the case, then round up to the nearest hundred *forints*. If no service charge has been tacked on, add 10 per cent and round up to the nearest hundred *forints*.

Sweet cakes are a Turkish legacy and Budapest has many family-run *cukrászda* (cake shops) offering these Turkish-inspired delights in winding forgotten alleyways all over town. When it's warm, there are plenty of cheap little outdoor fast-food stalls in the Városliget (City Park) serving *lángos* (ring-shaped savoury doughnuts), pretzels and corn on the cob to stave off your hunger pangs.

Pastries and breads are very popular in Hungary. From the crescent-shaped buttery, biscuity *kifli* to the filling nut rolls, most delis and corner shops will have a range on offer. Perfect for breakfast or as a snack during the day, you can even find shops selling tiny versions of each pastry, allowing you to 'pick and mix' your cakes.

USEFUL DINING PHRASES

I would like a table for ... people
Szeretnék egy asztalt ... személyre
Seh-reht-nayk ehdj os-tolt ... seh-mayy-reh

May I have the bill, please?
Kérhetem a számlát?
Kayr-heh-tehm o sahm-laht?

Waiter/Waitress!
Pincér/Pincérnő!
Pin-cayr/pin-cayr-nur!

Could I have it well cooked/medium rare, please?
Kaphatnám ezt jól megsülten/félig sülten?
Kop-hot-nahm ehzt johl mehg-shewl-tehn/ fay-leeg shewl-tehn?

I am a vegetarian. Does this contain meat?
Vegetáriánus vagyok. Van ebben hús?
Veh-geh-tah-ree-ah-nosh vodjok. Von ehb-behn hoosh?

Where is the toilet please?
Hol van a WC?
Hohl von o vay-tsay?

I would like a cup of/two cups of/another coffee/tea
Szeretnék egy csésze/két csésze kávét/még egy kávét/teát
Seh-reht-nayk ehdj chay-seh/kayt chay-she kah-veht/mayg ehdj kah-veht/teh-aht

Entertainment & nightlife

Budapest is open non-stop for a good time and offers something for everyone, from calm cafés to brash and bawdy transvestite shows. Most of the action happens in Pest: Liszt Ferenc tér and Ráday utca brim with fashionable venues and restaurants.

Be prepared to walk between venues, where you'll find jazz, blues, rock, disco, gypsy, Balkan and Hungarian folk music – all elbowing for your attention at the smoky, raucous clubs and bars. Most bars are open until 02.00; clubs continue until 04.00, though some stay open until dawn.

Budapest has a great club scene, featuring everything from hip-hop to salsa grooves, and the cover charges are very reasonable. One of the most original venues can be found at the Király Fürdő (King's Baths, see page 69). On regularly scheduled evenings, they turn into a steamy, trip-hop splash pad, with light reflecting off the steam as you groove in the water.

The *borozó* (wine cellar) is a Budapest institution. These smoky, cavernous rooms are usually filled with older men drinking cheap, but decent, wine and arguing over politics. Women, especially single women, will not feel welcome. The *söröző* (beer house) is more of a social place, where you can find good, affordable food and a more mixed group of locals, expats and foreign travellers.

If gambling's your thing, Budapest has over a dozen casinos, most of which are in the luxury hotels along the Duna korzó. Formal dress and a big wad of cash are often prerequisites for entry, though many now accept credit cards.

The Petőfi Csarnok (ⓐ XIV. Zichy Mihály út 14 ⓣ (01) 251 7266 ⓦ www.petoficsarnok.hu), in the Városliget, and the **Almássy téri Szabadidő Központ** (ⓐ VII. Almássy tér 6 ⓣ 70 278 6815 (mobile)

Metro: Blaha Lujzatér) are the two favourite venues for small pop concerts and folk music. International stars perform at the Puskás Ferenc Stadion, the main sports stadium, also known as Népstadion (see page 32). Purchase tickets for rock and jazz at **TEX Ticket Express** in Déli pályaudvar metro (VI. Andrássy út 18) and **Publika** (VII. Károly körút 9 Metro: Deák Ferenc tér).

The online resource www.caboodle.hu is probably the best source of nightlife listings in Budapest. English-speaking revellers will also want to pick up a copy of *Budapest Week* (www.budapestweek.com), *Budapest Funzine* (www.funzine.hu) or the *Budapest Sun* (www.budapestsun.com). *Where Budapest* is a useful monthly guide in English, available free at most hotels.

Fireworks over the Danube

Sport & relaxation

SPECTATOR SPORTS

Hungary's long and illustrious sporting tradition has sprouted more Olympic gold medallists per capita than any other country in the world. You may notice early in the mornings (on your way back from a night of clubbing) the throngs of schoolchildren who are forced into the water or on to the training field.

Although Hungarians are great individual athletes, they've had a hard time making it big in the world of team sports. Apathetic fans, corruption, underfunding and political problems have all contributed to the fact that Hungary's sporting teams haven't qualified for any major league championship since 1986. The football team **Ferencváros** (ⓦ www.ftc.hu) is the most successful club.

The best venue to view sporting events is the massive, Soviet-inspired **Puskás Ferenc Stadion** (ⓐ XIV. Istvánmezei út 1–3 ⓜ Metro: Stadionok).

PARTICIPATION SPORTS

Budapest is a big city and, even with a great metro system, you'll find your fitness level improved just by walking. Luckily, Budapest has some excellent parks and ambling spots. From Gellért Hill, you'll be treated to spectacular views of the city below, and as you walk along the Széchenyi rakpart leading to Margitsziget (Margaret Island, see page 109), you'll find boats moored on the quays with lots of cafés on board. Margaret Island is Budapest's playground that will exhaust you with opportunities to ride in a pedal car, toss a frisbee or jog on the cushioned path snaking round the island, while the Városliget (City Park, see page 93) is a great place to meander along the lake and go boating in summer or skating in winter.

Budapest Madness (www.budapestmadness.com) is a tour agency that specialises in hedonistic English-speaking group tours at very reasonable prices. They organise a heap of fun programmes that include Trabant (a funny little East German car that was popular during the Communist regime) rallies, thermal-bath crawls and helicopter tours over the city.

RELAXATION

The most tranquil way to relax in Budapest is to head to one of the city's baths. Try the Gellért Fürdő (Gellért Baths, see page 67) or the Széchenyi Baths (see page 46), not only to soak tired muscles, but also to lift your spirits after a long night out on the town.

Locals ice-skating next to Buda Castle

Accommodation

Budapest boasts some excellent accommodation options for the visitor. Whether you're into luxurious hotels offering bathing cures, chic self-catering apartments, funky budget digs or campsites, Budapest has it all.

Central Pest is where you'll find some of the nicest hotels, but they do come at a premium. If money is tight, try the outskirts of town. Good public transport allows easy access to the city centre.

The boom of renovation has had a definite effect on the quality of rooms. Many 3-star hotels are well designed and provide amenities such as international TV stations, Internet access, lifts, laundry and air conditioning. All hotels in Hungary are obliged to have a certain number of non-smoking rooms.

Hungarian *panzió* (bed and breakfasts) are family-run places with a personal touch. However, that personal touch may scream 'kitsch disaster', so ask to see a room before you commit.

Renting a self-catering apartment in the centre of town is a great way to save money and feel local. Use a reputable agency, such as IBUSZ (see page 119) or **OHB** (W www.ohb.hu). Good deals can sometimes be made with a tout at the railway station, but ask to see a map to check the location before you go traipsing off into the sunset.

PRICE CATEGORIES

This selection of accommodation is rated by price for a double room including breakfast.

£ up to 15,000 HUF **££** 15,000–30,000 HUF **£££** over 30,000 HUF

Camping is excellent in Buda – the grass is definitely greener a short distance from the hectic pace of town. Be sure not to pitch your tent illegally in any of Budapest's green areas, however, or you will be fined.

You can find more information about accommodation online at Ⓦ www.hotelinfo.hu, Ⓦ www.hotels.hu or the **Hungarian National Tourist Board** site (Ⓦ www.hungarytourism.hu). Once you're in town, your best bet is to go to one of the Tourinform offices (see page 153). IBUSZ is happy to book you into any hotel, apartment or hostel, and they don't charge a booking fee.

HOTELS

Ábel Pension £ Homespun charm in a restored family villa in the foothills of Gellért Hill. Ⓐ XI. Ábel Jenö útca 9 Ⓣ (1) 209 2537 Ⓦ www.abelpanzio.hu

easyHotel Budapest Oktogon £ Basic but in a prime position and good value for money. Ⓐ VI. Eötvös utca 25/a Ⓣ 20 469 8704 (mobile) Ⓦ www.easyhotel.com

Baross Hotel ££ A peaceful hotel with many light and airy rooms facing on to a typical Hungarian courtyard. Ⓐ VII. Baross utca 15 Ⓣ (1) 461 3010 Ⓦ www.barosshotel.hu

Boat Hotel Fortuna ££ A converted river cruiser turned mini luxury liner, with wood panelling, brass fittings, chandeliers and an English pub. Cheaper hostel accommodation with shared bathroom facilities in the hull, so you can get that touch of class for less. Ⓐ XIII. Szent István körút, Budai Alsó rakpart Ⓣ (1) 288 8100 Ⓦ www.fortunahajo.hu

City Hotel Pilvax ££ It's worth persevering with this hotel's website for quality, air-conditioned and central rooms. ⓐ V. Pilvax köz 1–3 ⓣ (1) 266 7660 ⓦ www.cityhotels.hu

Hotel Benczúr ££ A large hotel with modern rooms, apartments and suites and a minimalist 1970s approach in many of the common areas. ⓐ VI. Benczúr utca 35 ⓣ (1) 479 5650 ⓦ www.hotelbenczur.hu

Hotel Castle Garden ££ A new, environmentally friendly hotel in the heart of Buda's castle district. ⓐ I. Lovas útca 41 ⓣ (1) 224 7420 ⓦ www.hotelcastlegarden.hu

Leó Panzió ££ Excellent value in central Pest, this hotel occupies a traditional city building and boasts spacious rooms and friendly staff. ⓐ V. Kossuth Lajos utca 2/a ⓣ (1) 266 9041 ⓦ www.leopanzio.hu

Atrium £££ A contemporary fashion hotel. Dead central and dead stylish, but some rooms are noisy. ⓐ VII. Csokonai utca 14 ⓣ (1) 299 0777 ⓦ www.atriumhotelbudapest.com

Danubius Hotel Gellért £££ This superbly located hotel may enjoy spectacular Danube views but its glory has otherwise faded. Guests do however have access to the celebrated Gellért Baths (see page 67). ⓐ XI. Szent Gellért tér 1 ⓣ (1) 889 5500 ⓦ www.danubiushotels.com/gellert

Lánchíd 19 £££ A hotel with an award-winning design, affording some of the best views seen from a bathtub in the city. ⓐ I. Lánchíd utca 19–21 ⓣ (1) 419 1900 ⓦ www.lanchid19hotel.hu

The City Hotel Pilvax enjoys a central but quiet location

Faded glory at Danubius Hotel Gellért

Mercure Korona £££ Well-located, large hotel with excellent facilities and a mellow, street-level lounge. Take a dip in the pool to cool off. ⓐ V. Kecskeméti utca 14 ⓣ (1) 486 8800 ⓦ www.mercure-korona.hu

New York Palace £££ Italian splendour in a beautifully restored building. The spa, which was designed to represent an ice cave, is perfect as a respite from the Hungarian summer heat. ⓐ VI. Erzsébet körút 9–11 ⓣ (1) 886 6111 ⓦ www.boscolohotels.com

HOSTELS

Amigo Hostel £ A new location but still friendly, good value and central. ⓐ VII. Károly körút 5 (Bell 38) ⓣ 20 332 6322 (mobile) ⓦ www.amigohostel.hu

Art Guest House £ A clean, friendly hostel set around a gorgeous courtyard. It has a central location (next to Nyugati railway station)

and, although mattresses can be thin, there is a refreshing absence of bunk beds. ⓐ V. Podmaniczky utca 19 (doorbell ART) ⓣ (1) 302 3739 ⓦ www.arthostel.hu

Citadella Hotel and Hostel £ Great views and atmosphere atop Gellért Hill in an historic fortress. Twelve rooms and one 14-bed dorm. ⓐ XI. Citadella sétány ⓣ (1) 466 5794 ⓦ www.citadella.hu

Hostel Marco Polo £ Probably the cleanest and friendliest hostel in town. Doubles, quads and roomy dorms on offer with a pleasant courtyard, cheap Internet facilities and a bar. ⓐ VII. Nyár utca 6 ⓣ (1) 413 2555 ⓦ www.marcopolohostel.com

Loft £ Relaxed and charming hostel run by gourmands willing to barter discounts in return for hard-to-find delicacies. ⓐ V. Veres Pálné útca 19 ⓣ (1) 328 0916 ⓦ www.lofthostel.hu

Red Bus Hostel £ A centrally located, reasonably priced hostel, with its own second-hand English bookshop. ⓐ V. Semmelweis utca 14 ⓣ (1) 266 0136 ⓦ www.redbusbudapest.hu

CAMPSITES

Plan on spending about 2,500 HUF to pitch your tent and 3,500 HUF to park your caravan. There are several campsites in Budapest, but for the location and amenities (such as laundry facilities and pool), and friendly service, **Római Kemping** (ⓐ III. Szentendrei út 189 ⓣ (1) 388 7176 ⓦ www.romaicamping.hu) is the best place to rest. Other popular campsites include **Budapest Camping** (ⓐ X. Pilisi utca 7 ⓣ 30 296 9129 (mobile) ⓦ www.budapestcamping.hu) and **Zugligeti Niche Camping** (ⓐ XII. Zugligeti út 101 ⓣ (1) 200 8346 ⓦ www.campingniche.hu).

THE BEST OF BUDAPEST

Whether you're on a flying visit to Budapest, or taking a more leisurely break in Hungary, the city offers sights and experiences that should not be missed.

TOP 10 ATTRACTIONS

- **Országház (Houses of Parliament)** Laid languidly along the banks of the Danube, the city's political powerhouse seems to possess a spire for every day of the year (see page 80).

- **Houses of Worship** Szent István Bazilika (St Stephen's Basilica), Mátyás Templom (Matthias Church) and Nagy Zsinagóga (Great Synagogue) – superlative-filled houses of God reflect the diverse paths of religion in Budapest (see pages 84, 66 and 96).

- **Budavári Sikló (Buda Castle Funicular)** Lends new meaning to the phrase 'hanging out' (see page 62).

- **Halászbástya (Fishermen's Bastion)** The bird's-eye view over Pest is stunning, and so is the neo-Romanesque structure that you mount to enjoy it (see page 65).

- **Váci utca and Fő utca** As Váci utca's vibe ebbs towards over-commercialisation, the city has pedestrianised Fő utca (Pest side), which is now attracting a great assortment of atmospheric cafés, bars, galleries and boutiques (see pages 90 and 100).

- **Gellért Fürdő (Gellért Baths)** Relaxing muscles that you didn't even know were tense while soaking up the traditional – nay, decadent – ambience of this Art Nouveau lounge-arama really is the only sensible way of purging yourself of that last scintilla of stress (see page 67).

- **Margitsziget (Margaret Island)** This smack-in-the-middle-of-the-Danube outpost of paradise contains what must be Budapest's zenith of kitsch – a fountain that erupts to the sound of (badly) recorded muzak (see page 109).

- **Magyar Nemzeti Galéria (Hungarian National Gallery)** The most valuable collection of Hungarian art in the world (see page 69).

- **Állami Operaház (State Opera House)** Built to rival all great opera houses in its opulence, but actually offering affordable tickets, this hints at what the Communist experiment could have been like (see page 81).

- **Szoborpark (Statue Park)** Ha! Who needs Walt Disney's lovable mice when you can fill an entire theme park with reminders of those crazy days of Communist public art? Well, it's an angle... (see page 110).

Budapest's imposing Gothic Revival-style parliament building

Suggested itineraries

HALF-DAY: BUDAPEST IN A HURRY

Take the funicular up to the carefree and mostly car-free Castle district, a UNESCO World Heritage Site. If it's raining, take an hour to look at the world-renowned masterpieces at the Hungarian National Gallery (see page 69). From there, it's on to Buda Castle (see page 62) and the neo-Gothic Matthias Church (see page 66). Then, make your way to the sun-bleached Halászbástya (Fishermen's Bastion, see page 65) and climb the turrets, which afford possibly the finest views of Pest from across the Danube.

1 DAY: TIME TO SEE A LITTLE MORE

If you have a full day, walk along the embankment, admiring the boat traffic moving along the Danube as you cross Margit híd (Margaret Bridge). Pick up tram 2 at Jászai Mari tér, which will take you on a riverside circuit, passing some of the most important buildings of town. You'll take in the Országház (Houses of Parliament, see page 80), grand hotels such as Gresham Palace (see page 82) and, finally, the **Corvinus University of Budapest** (ⓦ www.uni-corvinus.hu). From there, you get a beautiful view of Gellért Hill across the Danube. Cross the Szabadság híd (Liberty Bridge) and end your day by visiting the Danubius Hotel Gellért, which has one of the most luxurious thermal baths in Budapest (see page 36). Walk back over the bridge to Pest and spend the evening window-shopping along Váci utca and Fő utca, the main pedestrianised shopping-friendly thoroughfares.

2–3 DAYS: TIME TO SEE MUCH MORE

To get a closer look at Budapest, you can see all the above sights, plus take in some other areas of interest. If the weather's nice, or you have

A view of Margaret Bridge from the Tabán

children, go to the Városliget (City Park, see page 93), which has some grandiose spaces to explore, including the Museum of Fine Arts (see page 94) and Hösök tere (Heroes' Square, see page 93), or to Margaret Island, a tranquil oasis in the middle of the Danube (see page 109).

LONGER: ENJOYING BUDAPEST TO THE FULL

With four or more days, you can see all the above sights, as well as climb Gellért Hill, stop off at the Sziklatemplom (Cave Church, see page 66) and go on to the Citadel (see page 65). With a bit more time, you'll be able to catch an opera performance in the evening or take a day trip to Hungary's favourite little town, Szentendre (see page 114).

Something for nothing

In Budapest, fun is fundamentally free. Catching trams 4 or 6 on Margaret Bridge will take you on a semicircular trip through the main areas of Pest, including Oktogon and Blaha Lujza tér; hopping on to tram 2 at Jászai Mari tér will take you on a grand tour of Budapest's main sights along the Danube for the price of a tram ticket. From there, try a little window-shopping along Váci utca, Budapest's pedestrian-friendly life vein. As you walk along, you can admire the buskers and street performers for, well, free.

Budapest is brimming with museums, with admission for adults ranging from only 800–1,200 HUF and some even offering free admission to permanent exhibitions. The most impressive include the free-entry **Magyar Nemzeti Múzeum** (**Hungarian National Museum** ⓐ VIII. Múzeum körút 14–16 ⓣ (1) 338 2122 ⓜ Metro: Kálvin tér), the Hungarian National Gallery (see page 69) and the Museum of Fine Arts (see page 94). Budapest's most beautiful churches are free to visit, including Szent István Bazilika (St Stephen's Basilica, see page 84), and you can even get a close look at the macabre sight of St Stephen's shrivelled-up forearm, displayed in a small glass cabinet. Other free entries include Cave Church (see page 66), hewn into the side of Gellért Hill by Pauline monks, and the Inner City Parish Church (see page 92), the oldest building in Pest.

For a unique insight into Hungarian history, visit **Kerepesi Cemetery** (ⓐ VIII Kerepesi temetõ ⓜ Metro: Keleti Pályaudvar). This is the final resting place of the famous and the revered; the cemetery is filled with elaborate statues, striking frescoes and massive mausoleums. It's a sober opportunity for historical, artistic and personal reflection.

Margaret Island (see page 109) is Budapest's playground, smack in the middle of the Danube. This 2.5 km (1½ miles) of gentle parks and

The Hungarian National Museum is just one of the many free museums

leafy picnic spots is part of the green belt of Budapest. Here you can wander the tree-lined paths, passing thermal spas, landmark monuments and ancient ruins. It's free to stick your toes in the water, but watch out for turtles, and there's also the dramatic water fountain that erupts sporadically into life against a backdrop of recorded classical music.

Entrance to Budapest's baths can cost anything up to 3,100 HUF. However, in many baths (including both the Gellért and Széchenyi baths), you receive money back if you leave before your time is up. So if you pay, say, 2,300 HUF to get into the Széchenyi Baths, and you leave within two hours, you will receive some money back on the way out; the amount depends on how long you've stayed.

When it rains

When it's raining cats and dogs, you have to think like a fish. The best way to beat the weather blues is to partake in one of Budapest's finest traditions ... the bath. Make your way either to the Gellért Baths (see page 67) or to the **Széchenyi Baths** (ⓐ XIV. Állatkerti körút 11 ⓣ (1) 363 3210 ⓦ www.spasbudapest.com) in the Városliget (City Park). This old complex of indoor and outdoor pools is the deepest, hottest and largest bathing facility in Budapest. After a good soak, you'll be ready to visit one of the beer houses nearby. One of the best beer houses in Budapest is **Bajor Sörsátor** (ⓐ XIV. Kós Károly sétány), where beer-drinking is considered a spectator sport, and wine is quaffed straight out of the barrel.

While you are around Városliget, drop into the Állatkert, or zoo (see page 148). It may seem like a strange choice, but there are plenty of exhibits inside and at least you won't have to worry about crowds. An exotic bird house, palm house, aquarium and indoor play area for children make this one of the best places to while away the bad weather.

If zoos aren't your thing, you could try a museum or two. Not far from the Városliget, you'll find two interesting museums where you can escape the dreary weather. The Museum of Fine Arts (see page 94) houses the largest collection of international art in Hungary. Rumour has it that there are more El Grecos here than in Spain. The House of Terror Museum (see page 98) is definitely the kind of place you want to visit on a miserable day. This award-winning controversial exhibition memorialises the cruelties committed during the German and Soviet occupations of Hungary.

When the heavens open, it's time to head underground. Pálvölgyi Stalactite Cave (see page 109) is resplendent with fossils, aragonite crystals and coffee-coloured stalactites. The thermal waters channelled through the stone also create gorgeous graduations of colour in the walls. Tours take place regularly throughout the day and a guide reveals how once upon a time, Hungary was underwater. Ancient history and geography have never been so interesting.

Cinemas and indoor shopping centres also provide a welcome respite. The Westend City Center (see page 86) has more than 400 shops and services to keep you busy on a rainy day. The multiplex cinema shows new releases of English-language films.

So, you see, a rainy day needn't make you feel like a fish out of water; you just have to go with the flow.

Get wet indoors at the Gellért Baths

On arrival

TIME DIFFERENCE

Hungary follows Central European Time, which is one hour ahead of GMT.

ARRIVING

By air

Getting into Budapest from **Budapest Ferihegy Airport** (ⓐ 1675 Budapest Ferihegy ⓣ (1) 296 9696 ⓦ www.bud.hu) is a piece of cake. The easiest way to get into town is by the **Airport Minibus** (ⓣ (1) 296 8555 ⓦ www.airportshuttle.hu). As you exit the arrivals hall, go up to the counter, give them your name and desired location, and they will pack you on your way in air-conditioned comfort. Save more money by booking a return ticket (single approximately 3,000 HUF, return approximately 5,000 HUF). On your return, book the Airport Minibus 24 hours in advance.

A taxi from the airport costs only a tad more and some taxi firms offer fixed prices from the airport to town. **Tele5Taxi** (ⓣ (1) 555 5555) charges approximately 5,000 HUF for a single journey and can often be found waiting outside the airport. Alternatively, try **City Taxi** (ⓣ (1) 211 1111) or **Fő Taxi** (ⓣ (1) 222 2222), both of which have similar fixed rates.

The bus from the airport is by far the cheapest option and will quickly familiarise you with the public transport system. When exiting the airport, find the bus stop that says 'BKV Plusz Reptér busz'. The bus stops at the airport every 15 minutes, from 04.55 to 23.20. It goes to Kőbánya-Kispest metro station (on the blue line), 20 minutes away. From there, take the metro into town. This takes 20 to 25 minutes to reach Deák Ferenc tér in central Pest. Purchase bus tickets from the orange vending machines outside Terminal 2A or next to the stop, or from the newspaper kiosk inside Terminal 2B.

By rail

Budapest has three major railway stations: **Déli pályaudvar** (ⓐ I. Krisztina körút 37 ⓣ (1) 375 6593) – the southern railway station; **Keleti pályaudvar** (ⓐ VIII. Rákóczi út ⓣ (1) 413 4610) – the eastern railway station; and **Nyugati pályaudvar** (ⓐ VI. Nyugati tér ⓣ (1) 349 8503) – the western railway station, which also has a rail connection to Ferihegy Airport Terminal 1. Each is conveniently connected to the metro system as well as to other public transport. All have bureaux de change, left-luggage facilities, public phones and information desks. For any information about the stations or timetable, call ⓣ 06 40 494 949 for English and Hungarian speakers, or, from abroad, call ⓣ +36 1 444 4499.

Budapest has the oldest metro system in continental Europe

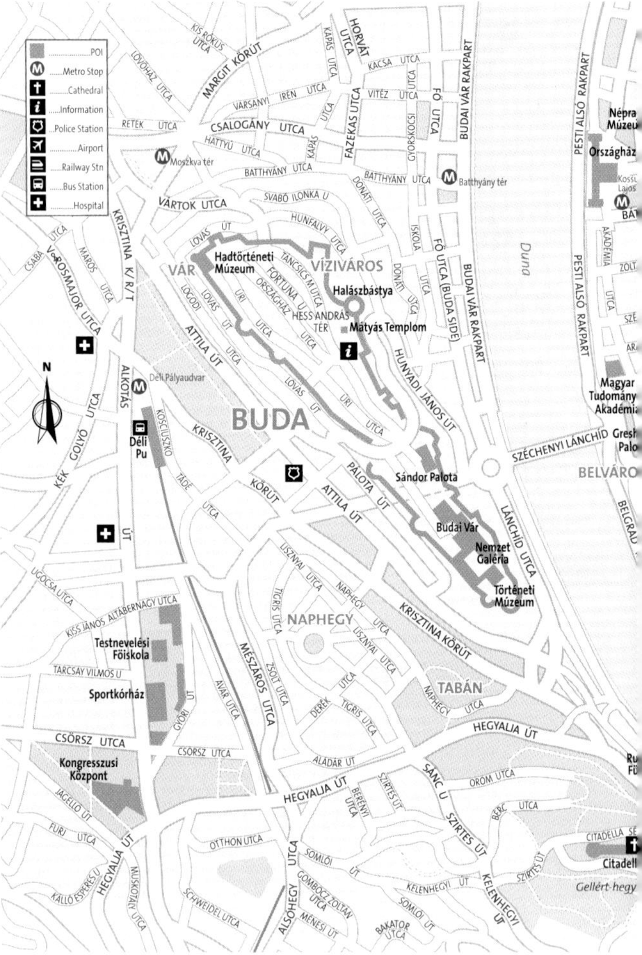
POI
Metro Stop
Cathedral
Information
Police Station
Airport
Railway Stn
Bus Station
Hospital
N
BUDA
VÁR
VÍZIVÁROS
NAPHEGY
TABÁN
BELVÁROS
Duna
Hadtörténeti Múzeum
Halászbástya
Mátyás Templom
Sándor Palota
Budai Vár
Nemzet Galéria
Történeti Múzeum
Moszkva tér
Batthyány tér
Déli Pályaudvar
Déli Pu
Testnevelési Föiskola
Sportkórház
Kongresszusi Központ
Citadell
Gellért-hegy
Országház
Magyar Tudomány Akadémia
MARGIT KÖRÚT
CSALOGÁNY UTCA
BATTHYÁNY UTCA
VÁRTOK UTCA
KRISZTINA K/R/T
KRISZTINA KÖRÚT
ATTILA ÚT
HUNYADI JÁNOS ÚT
BUDAI VÁR RAKPART
PESTI ALSÓ RAKPART
SZÉCHENYI LÁNCHÍD
LÁNCHÍD UTCA
HEGYALJA ÚT
ALKOTÁS ÚT
CSÖRSZ UTCA
MÉSZÁROS UTCA
FŐ UTCA
FŐ UTCA (BUDA SIDE)
FAZEKAS UTCA
HORVÁT UTCA
KÉK GOLYÓ UTCA
VÁROSMAJOR UTCA
PALOTA ÚT
SÁNC U
SZIRTES ÚT
KELENHEGYI ÚT
ALSÓHEGY UTCA
OTTHON UTCA
SOMLÓI ÚT
ALADÁR UT
TIGRIS UTCA
HESS ANDRÁS TÉR
LOVAS ÚT
ÚRI UTCA
FORTUNA U
ORSZÁGHÁZ UTCA
TÁNCSICS M UTCA
DONÁTI UTCA
ISKOLA
GYORSKOCSI UTCA
KACSA UTCA
VITÉZ UTCA
IRÉN UTCA
VARSÁNYI
HATTYÚ UTCA
KAPÁS UTCA
RETEK UTCA
SVÁBÓ ILONKA U
HUNFALVY UTCA
KISS JÁNOS ALTÁBERNAGY UTCA
TARCSAY VILMOS U
GYŐRI ÚT
AVAR UTCA
JAGELLÓ ÚT
FURJ UTCA
KOSCIUSZKO
LISZNYAI UTCA
NAPHEGY UTCA
DERÉK UTCA
ZSOLT UTCA
ORÓM UTCA
BÉRC UTCA
CITADELLA SÉ
SZIRTES ÚT
BERÉNYI UTCA
GOMBOCZ ZOLTÁN UTCA
MÉNESI ÚT
BAKATOR UTCA
SCHWEIDEL UTCA
KÁLLÓ ESPERES U
MUSKOTÁLY UTCA
UGOCSA UTCA
LOGODI
LÖVŐHÁZ UTCA
KIS RÓKUS UTCA
MAROS UTCA
CSABA UTCA

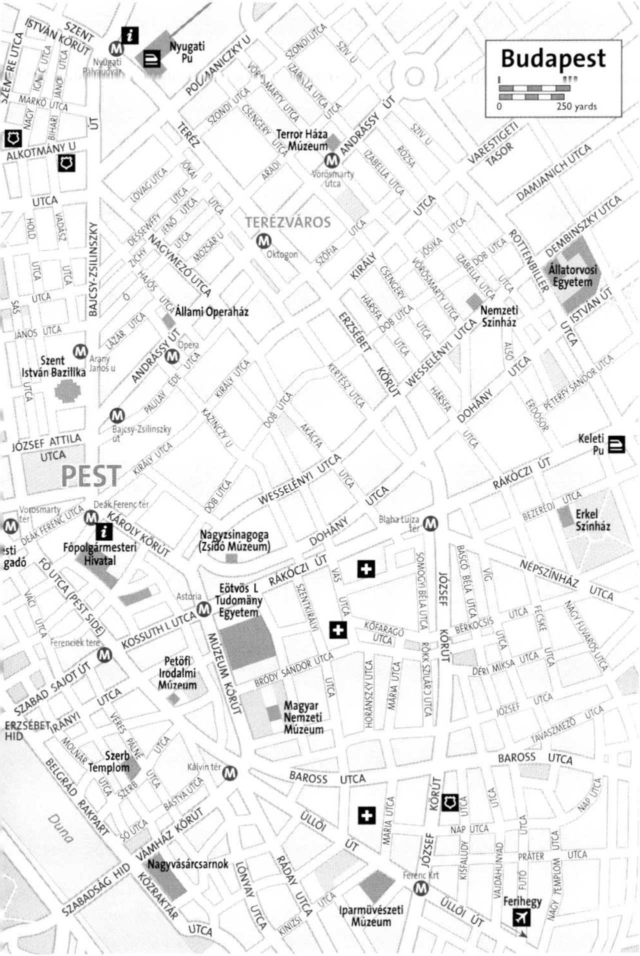
Budapest
0
250 yards
PEST
TERÉZVÁROS
Nyugati Pu
Nyugati Pályaudvar
Terror Háza Múzeum
Vörösmarty utca
Oktogon
Állami Operaház
Opera
Arany János u
Szent István Bazilika
Bajcsy-Zsilinszky út
Állatorvosi Egyetem
Nemzeti Színház
Keleti Pu
Erkel Színház
Blaha Lujza tér
Vörösmarty tér
Deák Ferenc tér
Fópolgármesteri Hivatal
Nagyzsinagoga (Zsidó Múzeum)
Eötvös L Tudomány Egyetem
Astória
Ferenciek tere
Petőfi Irodalmi Múzeum
Magyar Nemzeti Múzeum
Szerb Templom
Kálvin tér
Nagyvásárcsarnok
Iparmüvészeti Múzeum
Ferenc Krt
Ferihegy
Duna
ANDRÁSSY ÚT
RÁKÓCZI ÚT
ÜLLŐI ÚT
BAROSS UTCA
MÚZEUM KÖRÚT
KÁROLY KÖRÚT
ERZSÉBET KÖRÚT
JÓZSEF KÖRÚT
VÁMHÁZ KÖRÚT
BAJCSY-ZSILINSZKY ÚT
WESSELÉNYI UTCA
DOHÁNY UTCA
KOSSUTH L UTCA
SZABADSÁG HÍD
ERZSÉBET HÍD
BELGRÁD RAKPART
KÖZRAKTÁR UTCA
NÉPSZÍNHÁZ UTCA
ISTVÁN ÚT
DAMJANICH UTCA
DEMBINSZKY UTCA
VÁRESTIGETI TASOR
ROTTENBILLER UTCA
KIRÁLY UTCA
NAGYMEZŐ UTCA
TERÉZ KÖRÚT
PODMANICZKY U
SZENT ISTVÁN KÖRÚT
ALKOTMÁNY U
JÓZSEF ATTILA UTCA
FŐ UTCA (PEST SIDE)
RÁDAY UTCA
LÓNYAY UTCA
SZABAD SAJTÓ ÚT

By road

The M0 circles Budapest with the M1, M3, M5 and M7 toll motorways linking drivers to the city from all directions. Driving in Budapest isn't recommended, as many of the thoroughfares near the sights and tourist areas are pedestrian-only. Park your car in one of the many centrally located multi-storey car parks, and you'll be well on your way.

If you get into car trouble, the **Hungarian Automobile Club** (t (1) 345 1800) offers 24-hour roadside assistance and emergency roadside help (t 188).

FINDING YOUR FEET

Let's face it – Budapest is big. But it's beautiful in the way that it routes heavy traffic around the centre, making many of the centrally located tourist sections an ambler's heaven. It's also heaven for

Use the Danube to find your bearings

pickpockets, so keep your valuables at your side and don't let yourself get too distracted by the beautiful scenery. The cobbled streets can play havoc with heels so wear comfortable shoes.

ORIENTATION

The Duna (Danube) runs north–south through Budapest, separating the city into Buda (to the west) and Pest (to the east). For bucolic beauty, quiet streets and great views, head for the hills – the Buda Hills, that is. For the glitz and glamour of city life, go to Pest. Some of the most striking architecture in Budapest is along the Danube, which is perfect for strolling.

The best way to get your bearings is to walk along the Danube embankment, on the Pest side, from Március 15 tér to Roosevelt tér. Outdoor cafés and benches sprawl out next to hotel fronts with great views of Castle Hill, looming over the other side of the Danube. Sitting on the railings along the tram line at Vigadó tér is the statue of the

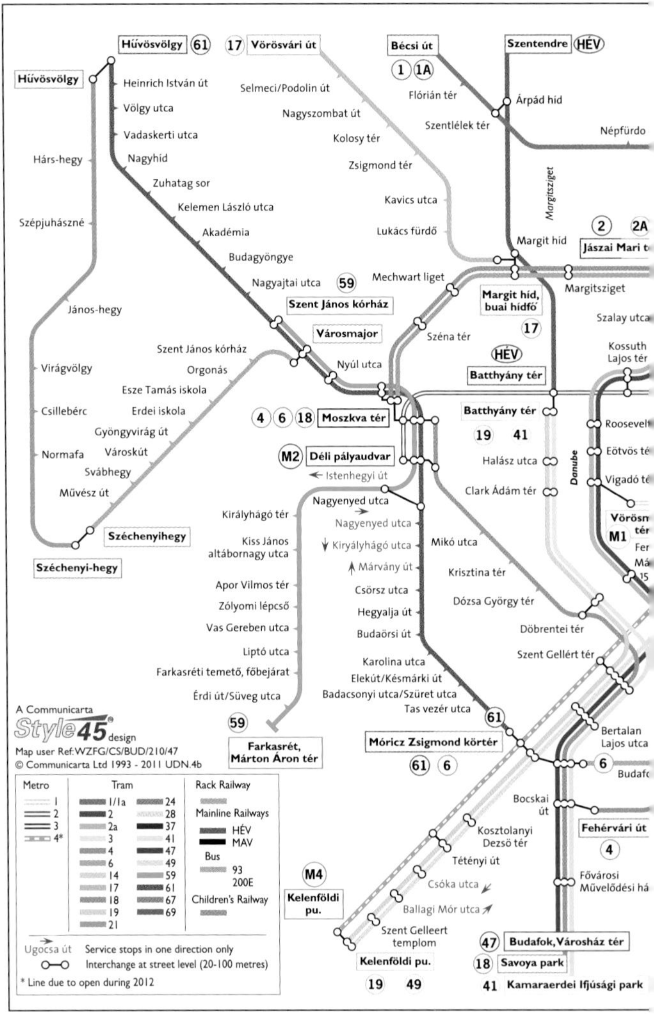
Hűvösvölgy
61
17
Vörösvári út
Bécsi út
Szentendre
HÉV
Hűvösvölgy
Heinrich István út
Völgy utca
Vadaskerti utca
Nagyhíd
Zuhatag sor
Kelemen László utca
Akadémia
Budagyöngye
Nagyajtai utca
Selmeci/Podolin út
Nagyszombat út
Kolosy tér
Zsigmond tér
Kavics utca
Lukács fürdő
1
1A
Flórián tér
Szentlélek tér
Árpád híd
Népfürdo
Margitsziget
Margit híd
2
2A
Jászai Mari t
Margitsziget
Hárs-hegy
Szépjuhászné
János-hegy
Virágvölgy
Csillebérc
Normafa
59
Szent János kórház
Mechwart liget
Margit híd, buai hídfő
17
Szalay utca
Városmajor
Széna tér
Szent János kórház
Orgonás
Nyúl utca
HÉV
Batthyány tér
Kossuth Lajos tér
Esze Tamás iskola
Erdei iskola
Gyöngyvirág út
Városkút
Svábhegy
Művész út
4
6
18
Moszkva tér
Batthyány tér
19
41
Roosevelt
Eötvös té
M2
Déli pályaudvar
Halász utca
Istenhegyi út
Clark Ádám tér
Danube
Vigadó té
Nagyenyed utca
Királyhágó tér
Nagyenyed utca
Vörösm tér
M1
Kiss János altábornagy utca
Kiryályhágó utca
Mikó utca
Fer
Má
15
Széchenyihegy
Széchenyi-hegy
Márvány út
Krisztina tér
Apor Vilmos tér
Csörsz utca
Zólyomi lépcső
Dózsa György tér
Hegyalja út
Vas Gereben utca
Budaörsi út
Döbrentei tér
Liptó utca
Szent Gellért tér
Karolina utca
Farkasréti temető, főbejárat
Elekút/Késmárki út
Érdi út/Süveg utca
Badacsonyi utca/Szüret utca
Tas vezér utca
61
Bertalan Lajos utca
A Communicarta
Style 45 design
Map user Ref:WZFG/CS/BUD/210/47
© Communicarta Ltd 1993 - 2011 UDN.4b
59
Farkasrét, Márton Áron tér
Móricz Zsigmond körtér
61
6
6
Budafo
Metro
1
2
3
4*
Tram
1/1a
2
2a
3
4
6
14
17
18
19
21
24
28
37
41
47
49
59
61
67
69
Rack Railway
Mainline Railways
HÉV
MAV
Bus
93
200E
Children's Railway
Ugocsa út
Service stops in one direction only
Interchange at street level (20-100 metres)
* Line due to open during 2012
Bocskai út
Kosztolanyi Dezsö tér
Fehérvári út
4
Tétényi út
M4
Kelenföldi pu.
Csóka utca
Ballagi Mór utca
Fővárosi Művelődési há
Szent Gelleert templom
47
Budafok, Városház tér
Kelenföldi pu.
18
Savoya park
19
49
41
Kamaraerdei Ifjúsági park

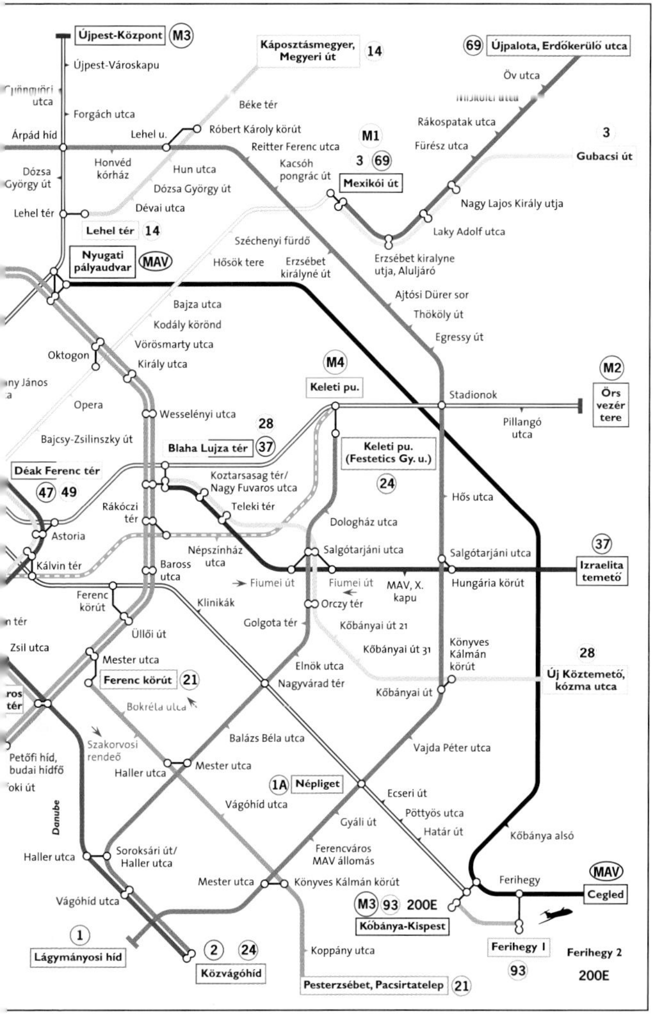
Újpest-Központ
M3
Újpest-Városkapu
utca
Forgách utca
Árpád híd
Lehel u.
Róbert Károly körút
Káposztásmegyer, Megyeri út
14
Béke tér
69
Újpalota, Erdőkerülő utca
Öv utca
Rákospatak utca
Fűrész utca
3
Gubacsi út
M1
3 69
Mexikói út
Reitter Ferenc utca
Kacsóh pongrác út
Honvéd kórház
Hun utca
Dózsa György út
Dózsa György út
Dévai utca
Lehel tér
Lehel tér 14
Nagy Lajos Király utja
Laky Adolf utca
Erzsébet kiralyne utja, Aluljáró
Széchenyi fürdő
Hősök tere
Erzsébet királyné út
Nyugati pályaudvar
MAV
Ajtósi Dürer sor
Thököly út
Egressy út
Bajza utca
Kodály köröndd
Vörösmarty utca
Oktogon
Király utca
M4
Keleti pu.
M2
Örs vezér tere
Stadionok
Pillangó utca
Opera
Wesselényi utca
28
Bajcsy-Zsilinszky út
Blaha Lujza tér 37
Keleti pu. (Festetics Gy. u.)
24
Déak Ferenc tér
47 49
Koztarsasag tér/ Nagy Fuvaros utca
Teleki tér
Rákóczi tér
Hős utca
Dologház utca
Astoria
Népszínház utca
Salgótarjáni utca
Salgótarjáni utca
37
Izraelita temető
Kálvin tér
Baross utca
Fiumei út
Fiumei út
MAV, X. kapu
Hungária körút
Ferenc körút
Klinikák
Orczy tér
Üllői út
Golgota tér
Kőbányai út 21
Zsil utca
Kőbányai út 31
Könyves Kálmán körút
28
Mester utca
Elnök utca
Ferenc körút 21
Nagyvárad tér
Új Köztemető, kózma utca
Kőbányai út
Bokréla utca
Szakorvosi rendeő
Balázs Béla utca
Vajda Péter utca
Petőfi híd, budai hídfő
Haller utca
Mester utca
1A Népliget
Ecseri út
Vágóhíd utca
Pöttyös utca
Danube
Határ út
Gyáli út
Kőbánya alsó
Haller utca
Soroksári út/ Haller utca
Ferencváros MAV állomás
Ferihegy
MAV
Cegled
Mester utca
Könyves Kálmán körút
Vágóhíd utca
M3 93 200E
Kőbánya-Kispest
1
Lágymányosi híd
2 24
Közvágóhíd
Koppány utca
Ferihegy I
Ferihegy 2
93
200E
Pesterzsébet, Pacsirtatelep 21

MAKING SENSE OF BUDAPEST ADDRESSES

Addresses in Budapest are as clear as, well, Hungarian, but there's a method to what seems to be madness. Budapest addresses begin with the number of the district. There are 23 districts in Budapest, labelled in Roman numerals, the most central being the I., V. and VII. (first, fifth and seventh) districts. Take, for example, V. Petőfi tér. Petőfi tér is the street name, and it's in the V. district, so you know it's central. '*Tér*' means 'square', while '*utca*' means 'street' and '*út*' means 'road', so be clear as to whether you're heading for a street or a road – there is the tourist strip of Váci utca but also a pretty dull Váci út, both of which are in Pest.

In a typical Budapest home address, a combination of three numerals then follows the street name, for example, Kossuth Lajos utca 14. III. 24. The first numeral after the street name denotes the number of the apartment building, the second numeral the number of the floor and the third numeral the number of the individual apartment. Confusingly, some old buildings in Pest are designated as having a half-floor, or upper-ground floor, between the ground and first floor proper – so what the British would call the second floor, and Americans the third, Hungarians might describe as the first.

'Little Princess'. From there, make your way to either Váci utca or Fő utca (Pest side). These chic pedestrianised streets are the heart of Budapest, perfect for window-shopping and people-watching. Buy a large map of the town, sit down at one of the many comfortable cafés and plan your visit. Otherwise, take tram 4 or 6 from Margaret Bridge, which will take you on a very cheap, semicircular tour of Pest.

GETTING AROUND

Public transport has a long history in Budapest; it has the oldest metro system in continental Europe. Luckily, all of Budapest's treasures are easily accessible on foot or by the **Budapest Public Transport Company** (BKV, www.bkv.hu). The BKV operates metro lines (M1, yellow; M2, red; M3, blue), blue local buses, yellow trams and red trolleybuses, which generally run from 04.30 to 23.00. Prior to boarding, purchase your tickets at metro stations, newsagents or hotels. You must validate your tickets in a ticket puncher and present them, upon request, to an inspector. It makes no sense to ride without a valid ticket; inspectors check tickets frequently on all lines, stepping on to the bus or tram wearing casual clothes and then putting on their official armband and badges. If you buy the Budapest Card (see page 18), then your travel on all public transport is covered; if you're not interested in the Budapest Card, then it's more economical to buy one of the one-, three- or seven-day metro passes (from 1,550 HUF) or a book of ten tickets (2,350 HUF), so that you're not constantly fishing around for change.

IF YOU GET LOST, TRY ...

Excuse me, do you speak English?
Elnézést, beszél angolul?
Ehl-nay-zaysht, beh-sayl on-goh-lool?

Can you point to it on my map?
Meg tudná ezt mutatni a térképemen?
Mehg tood-nah ehzt moo-tot-nee o tayr-kay-peh-mehn?

If you're over 65 and an EU citizen, you can ride the HÉV trains for free. You will need to show proof of identification, so if you look fifty-something rather than sixty-something, it's best to keep your passport to hand. Similarly, all EU citizens under the age of 26 can get discounted train travel on weekends.

Taking a taxi is simple. By law, taxis cannot charge more than the following amounts anywhere in Budapest: from 06.00–22.00, a 300-HUF basic fee, then 240 HUF for each additional one km (half-mile) or 60 HUF a minute. Waiting costs 70 HUF per minute. From 22.00–06.00, the price increases to a 420 HUF basic fee, then 336 HUF for each additional one km (half-mile), or 84 HUF a minute.

All taxis must have working meters and be able to issue a receipt. City Taxi and Fő Taxi (see page 48) have a trustworthy reputation. Taxi drivers will expect a small tip at the end of the journey. Add 10 per cent and round up to the nearest hundred *forints*.

Car hire

Hiring a car in Budapest makes no sense, unless you're planning to take a trip out into the country. For the best discounts (up to 50 per cent, in some cases), you need to book ahead and online. The following companies have offices in the airport and in town, and are generally open from Monday to Friday, from 08.00 to 20.00.

Budget Rent a Car ⓣ (1) 214 0420 ⓦ www.budget.hu

Europcar Inc ⓣ (1) 421 8333 ⓦ www.europcar.hu

FOX Autorent Owned and run by Hungarians; cheaper than the big guys ⓣ (1) 382 9000 ⓦ www.fox-autorent.com

Hertz ⓣ (1) 296 0999 ⓦ www.hertz.hu

Kemwel ⓦ www.kemwel.com

The newly restored roof of Matthias Church

THE CITY OF
Budapest

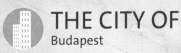

Buda: the Castle District, Gellért Hill & Tabán

These three small districts in Buda contain a textbook's worth of historical sights and are a stronghold of the Hungarian psyche: strong enough to look back into the treachery of the past, smart enough to continue forward. This area of town is now home to some of Budapest's most sought-after addresses and swankiest restaurants.

A UNESCO World Heritage Site, Buda is the *grande dame* of Budapest, surviving at all costs. Its streets are filled with ivy-clad history, vista-rich villas, Gothic arches, and hired horsemen with carriages and tourists, lots of them. It's no wonder; you really can't visit Budapest without spending time in the Castle District, to see where it all began. Buda is an ancient Slavic word meaning 'hut' or 'small dwelling', and that's what originally stood in this area until the arrival of the Mongols in the 13th century. King Béla built the first fortress here, a stronghold that has been rebuilt several times throughout history with the invasions of Turks and Habsburgs. It still bears the bullet scars of the last conflict in 1945 as the Germans retreated.

When the pope sent Bishop Gellért to oversee the coronation of King Stephen (later, St Stephen), and to convert the wayward Magyars, he was greeted very differently than he expected. The ungrateful masses tossed Bishop Gellért down the hill in a spiked barrel. At the top of Gellért Hill, the Felszabadulási Emlékmű (Liberation Monument) stands (see page 65), created to honour Soviet soldiers who 'liberated' Hungary from the Germans. Even further uphill is the Citadel (see page 65), built by the Habsburgs to keep a watchful eye and maintain an intimidating presence over the city. The views from here are among the best in the city; join tourists and locals alike on the well-maintained walking paths.

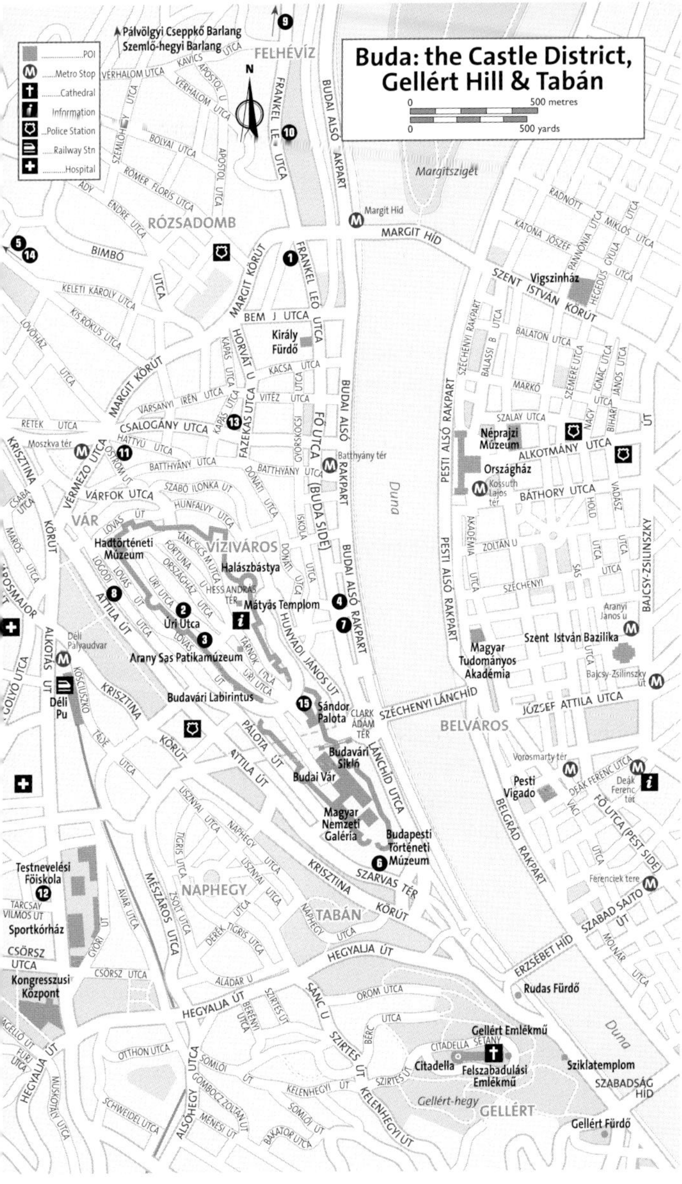

Buda: the Castle District, Gellért Hill & Tabán
0
500 metres
0
500 yards
POI
Metro Stop
Cathedral
Information
Police Station
Railway Stn
Hospital
N
Pálvölgyi Cseppkő Barlang
Szemlő-hegyi Barlang
FELHÉVÍZ
RÓZSADOMB
Margitsziget
Margit Híd
MARGIT HÍD
VÉRHALOM UTCA
KAVICS
APOSTOL U
BOLYAI UTCA
RÓMER FLÓRIS UTCA
FRANKEL LEÓ UTCA
BUDAI ALSÓ RAKPART
BIMBÓ
KELETI KÁROLY UTCA
KIS RÓKUS UTCA
MARGIT KÖRÚT
BEM J UTCA
Király Fürdő
KACSA UTCA
VITÉZ UTCA
HORVÁT U
FAZEKAS UTCA
CSALOGÁNY UTCA
RETEK UTCA
Moszkva tér
HATTYÚ UTCA
BATTHYÁNY UTCA
Batthyány tér
FŐ UTCA (BUDA SIDE)
VÁRFOK UTCA
VÁR
VÍZIVÁROS
Hadtörténeti Múzeum
Halászbástya
HESS ANDRÁS TÉR
Mátyás Templom
Úri Utca
Arany Sas Patikamúzeum
Budavári Labirintus
HUNYADI JÁNOS ÚT
Sándor Palota
CLARK ÁDÁM TÉR
SZÉCHENYI LÁNCHÍD
Budavári Sikló
Budai Vár
Magyar Nemzeti Galéria
Budapesti Történeti Múzeum
LÁNCHÍD UTCA
PÁLOTA ÚT
ATTILA ÚT
Déli Palyaudvar
Déli Pu
ALKOTÁS ÚT
KRISZTINA KÖRÚT
NAPHEGY
TABÁN
SZARVAS TÉR
Testnevelési Föiskola
Sportkórház
Kongresszusi Központ
MÉSZÁROS UTCA
HEGYALJA ÚT
Rudas Fürdő
ERZSÉBET HÍD
Gellért Emlékmű
CITADELLA SÉTÁNY
Citadella
Felszabadulási Emlékmű
Sziklatemplom
Gellért-hegy
GELLÉRT
SZABADSÁG HÍD
Gellért Fürdő
KELENHEGYI ÚT
SZIRTES ÚT
SÁNC U
Duna
PESTI ALSÓ RAKPART
SZENT ISTVÁN KÖRÚT
Vigszinház
Néprajzi Múzeum
ALKOTMÁNY UTCA
Országház
Kossuth Lajos tér
BÁTHORY UTCA
Szent István Bazilika
Aranyi János u
Magyar Tudományos Akadémia
Bajcsy-Zsilinszky út
BAJCSY-ZSILINSZKY ÚT
JÓZSEF ATTILA UTCA
BELVÁROS
Vorosmarty tér
Pesti Vigado
Deák Ferenc tér
DEÁK FERENC UTCA
FŐ UTCA (PEST SIDE)
BELGRÁD RAKPART
Ferenciek tere
SZABAD SAJTÓ ÚT

Tabán's terraced gardens of today hide the footsteps of Buda's founding fathers. On the site where Buda's first Celts settled, Romans dominated and Turks bathed, and where a slum inhabited by Serbs, Greeks and Gypsies once stood, Tabán is now a summer outdoor music venue.

The best way to reach this area is on the Buda Castle Funicular from Clark Adám tér. If you're more likely to feel vertiginous than thrilled by the view from the funicular, you can climb up the twisting walkway that leads from Clark Adám tér, or even take the lift from Dózsa György tér. Bus 16 runs from Deák Ferenc tér to Moszkva tér, and Bus 16A runs from here on a loop around the castle. Once you've made it, plan on a lot of easy ambling between sights.

SIGHTS & ATTRACTIONS

Budai Vár (Buda Castle)

Also known as the Royal Palace, Buda Castle in fact comprises several structures built and rebuilt over the centuries, after successive conflicts with the Turks, the Habsburgs and the Germans. The first castle dates from around 1255, but was reconstructed by King Matthias in 1458. During the Renaissance, the castle was at its architectural peak, with indoor plumbing and wine flowing from its fountains. All of this was destroyed during the Turkish siege of 1541. Reconstructed yet again after World War II, it now houses the Budapest History Museum and the Hungarian National Gallery (see page 69).

Budavári Sikló (Buda Castle Funicular)

First opened in 1870, this funicular railway was destroyed by the Germans in World War II. Lovingly restored in 1986, it continues to haul intrepid passengers from Clark Adám tér up to Buda

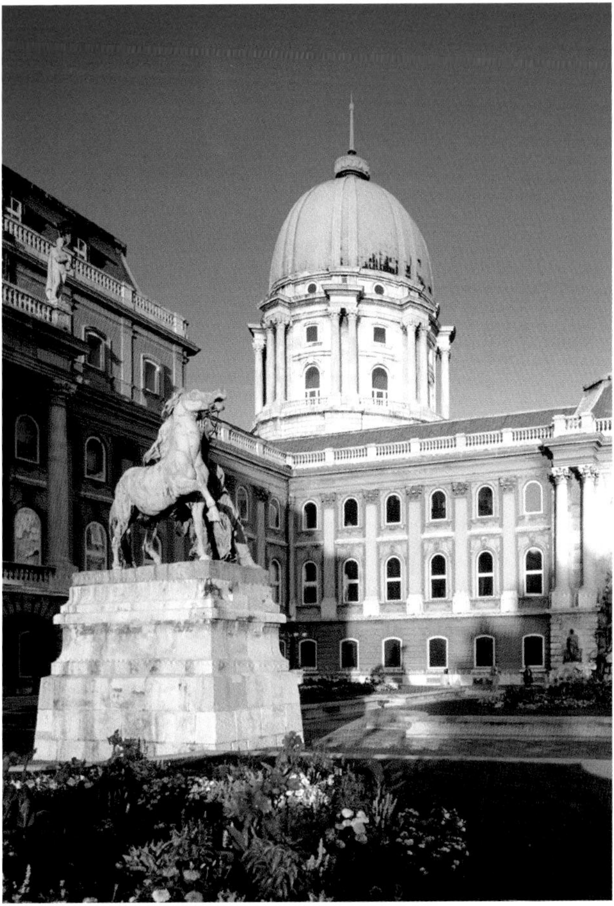

Buda Castle, the Royal Palace, has been sympathetically reconstructed

▲ *The Buda Castle Funicular climbs above the city*

Castle. You will get a great view of Pest and the Danube as you gain altitude. Admission charge

Citadella (Citadel)

On St Stephen's Day (20 August), the Hungarian army sets fireworks ablaze from this monument built by the Habsburgs after the 1848–9 uprising. Today it houses a youth hostel and nightclub, testament to the power that reigns over modern-day Budapest: tourism. www.citadella.hu

Felszabadulási Emlékmű (Liberation Monument)

This controversial statue of Lady Liberty perched atop the Citadel is one of the few remaining pieces of Soviet public art in Budapest. Originally commissioned to commemorate the city's 'liberation' by Soviet forces, it now honours all those who 'laid down their lives for Hungarian prosperity'.

Gellért Emlékmű (Gellért Monument)

This monument was erected in 1904 to atone for the sins of the fathers of Budapest, who, to renounce the Christian faith, pushed Bishop Gellért over the hill in a spiked barrel. Lit up at night, it's a beautiful beacon. To walk up to the monument, tram: 18, 19, 41, 47, 49 to Szent Gellért tér. To go straight to the top, tram to Móricz Zsigmond körtér followed by bus: 27

Halászbástya (Fishermen's Bastion)

A statue of St Stephen guards this neo-Romanesque structure. The view is stunning, especially in the early morning or late evening when the tourist hordes have diminished. It was built in 1895 as a monument to the Fishermen's Guild. 09.00–23.00 daily

Mátyás Templom (Matthias Church)
It's interesting to note that although the Hungarian King Matthias lent his name to this church built in 1470, Hungarians were not permitted to worship here. Germans worshipped at the church until the Turks came to power and converted it into a mosque. Legend has it that, in 1686, a vision of the Madonna appeared during prayers at the mosque. The Turks took the hint, and lost the city to the Habsburgs. ⓐ I. Szentháromság tér 2 ⓣ (1) 355 5657 ⓦ www.matyas-templom.hu ◔ 09.00–17.00 Mon–Fri, 09.00–12.00 Sat, 13.00–17.00 Sun ⓘ Admission charge (but not to under-sixes)

Sándor Palota (Alexander Palace)
This is the home of the Hungarian president. Unless you are on official business, you can't see the beauty that lies within. However, you can admire its neoclassical façade which was reconstructed after World War II. ⓐ I. Szent György tér 1

Sziklatemplom (Cave Church)
This church set in the cliffside was founded by Pauline monks in 1926. In the 1950s, the Communists put a stop to their Order, murdering the leader and sentencing the rest to prison. The church was bricked up and forgotten until August 1989, after the fall of the Communist regime. The result is spooky and strange, but worth the visit. ⓐ XI. Gellérthegy ◔ 09.00–11.00, 12.00–16.00 & 18.30–19.30 daily ⓣ Tram: 18, 19, 41, 47, 49 to Szent Gellért tér

Úri utca (Lords' Street)
Medieval-styled façades of houses built after the 1950s give this street, perfect for strolling, its special character. Highlights include No 9, where the Buda Castle Labyrinth begins, No 31 with Gothic

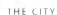

ornamentation, and No 49, which houses the **Telephone Museum** (see w www.budapestinfo.hu for information on opening hours).

CULTURE

Arany Sas Patikamúzeum (Golden Eagle Pharmaceutical Museum)
One of the oldest houses in the Castle District, this museum holds interesting exhibits of Hungarian pharmaceutical history, including an alchemical laboratory. It even has mummy powder from Transylvania. a I. Tárnok utca 18 t (1) 375 9772 10.00–18.00 Tues–Sun (Mar–Oct); 10.00–16.00 Tues–Sun (Nov–Feb)

Budapesti Történeti Múzeum (Budapest History Museum)
With artefacts, illustrations and photos of excavations, this museum traces the development of Budapest from the dawn of human history to the present day. Temporary rotating exhibitions fill out the experience nicely. a I. Szent György tér 2 w www.btm.hu 10.00–18.00 Tues–Sun (Mar–Oct); 10.00–16.00 Tues–Sun (Nov–Feb)

Budavári Labirintus (Buda Castle Labyrinth)
Used as an air-raid shelter during World War II, this network of caves and passageways houses a cheeky anti-art exhibition by Hungarian art students. The caves have been separated into chambers and halls, including the Renaissance Hall of Rocks with its novel ivy-covered fountain spouting red wine. a I. Úri utca 9 t (1) 212 0207 w www.labirintus.com 09.30–19.30 daily

Gellért Fürdő (Gellért Baths)
Renovated in 2007, these Art Deco baths are the best-known and probably the most luxurious in Budapest, with soaring columns,

MAKING THE MOST OF THE TURKISH BATHS

All of these baths have one thing in common: the Turks. When the Turks took Buda Castle in 1541, Buda became a Muslim city, the churches were converted to mosques and the natural limestone hot springs were made into traditional Turkish bathhouses that remain to this day. Each bath in Budapest has its own personality and set of bizarre rules, but the basic idea is the same.

A general entrance fee is all you need to make the most of the bathing experience. There are a gazillion other items on the menu, but most likely you will only want a massage and not a turbomatic skin slough. You pay for your massage (always given by a member of the same sex) at the ticket counter, for which you'll be given a token that you will then give to the masseur. Remember to tell them you don't speak Hungarian, so that they'll call your name out in English, or wave to you when it's your turn. When you hand your ticket to the bath attendant, you will get a silly-looking little cloth to tie around your waist. Women get some sort of apron-like covering for their breasts, but seldom use it. The idea is to move between pools and sauna, alternating temperatures from scalding hot to downright freezing until you find the right place to relax. At the end of your stay, you can relax in a resting room, before you put your street clothes back on.

You should bring your own towels and soap. The pools have separate areas for men, women and families, but most have a non-segregated pool. Lockers are free or cost a nominal fee and you can also pay extra for your own cabin. Note that if you stay under two hours, you will receive some money back.

Sampling the waters is the perfect way to indulge in a little bit of local culture. Bathing plays a big part in the Hungarian way of life and the thermal waters are said to ease all sorts of ailments, including arthritis and skin complaints. Go to Ⓦ www.spasbudapest.com for more information about the Budapest bathing experience.

stained-glass windows and an outdoor swimming pool with one of the world's first wave machines. Linger awhile in the splendour of the Viennese-style café, remembering when you're sipping your espresso that you owe it to the Turks. Ⓐ XI. Kelenhegyi út 4 Ⓣ (1) 466 6166 Ⓒ 08.00–20.00 daily

Király Fürdő (King's Baths)

Bask in glory under the towering dome in these baths and saunas which opened in 1566 for the Ottoman governor. Ⓐ II. Fő utca (Buda side) 82–84 Ⓣ (1) 201 3688 Ⓒ 08.00–20.00 daily Ⓘ Women only Mon & Wed; men only Tues & Thur–Sat; mixed Sun

Magyar Nemzeti Galéria (Hungarian National Gallery)

The very best of Hungarian creative arts can be found in the sumptuous rooms of this gallery, which is as much a work of art as the pieces hung on its walls. With collections ranging from medieval to contemporary, perhaps the strongest collection is from the 19th-century Secessionist movement, which pushed the boundaries into controversial subjects and the avant-garde. Ⓐ I. Dísz tér 17 Ⓦ www.mng.hu Ⓒ 10.00–18.00 Tues–Sun Ⓘ Admission to the permanent exhibitions is free

Rudas Fürdő (Rudas Baths)
After extensive renovations in 2005, Budapest's finest baths retain their glorious Ottoman flavour. Shafts of light cut through the gloom, as the domes reflect the chatter of bathers and splashing water.
ⓐ I. Döbrentei tér 9 ⓣ (1) 356 1322 ◷ 08.00–20.00 Mon–Thur, 08.00–20.00 & 22.00–04.00 Fri, 06.00–17.00 & 22.00–04.00 Sat, 06.00–17.00 Sun ⓘ Men only Mon & Wed–Fri (day); Women only Tues; mixed Fri (night), Sat & Sun. Fri & Sat nights are club nights with music

RETAIL THERAPY

This area is not so much a shopping district as an atmospheric, impulse-buy district. For serious shopping, or on a rainy day, go to **Mammut** (ⓐ II. Lövőház utca 2–6 ⓣ (1) 345 8020 ⓦ www.mammut.hu ⓜ Metro: Moszkva tér), two massive complexes in Buda that not only house more than 300 top-name fashion shops, but also have Internet access, bowling, casinos, amusement arcades, cinemas, dance clubs and fitness studios. Gastronomes will appreciate the stylish restaurants and cafés in the surrounding area.

Auguszt Cukrászda A quaint family-owned business that just happens to supply some of the best cakes in town. ⓐ I. Fény utca 8 ⓣ (1) 316 3817 ◷ 10.00–18.00 Tues–Fri, 09.00–18.00 Sat ⓜ Metro: Moszkva tér

Budapest Wine Society This is the place to sample the best local Hungarian wines. They stock hundreds of varieties, including rare and special vintages. ⓐ I. Batthyány utca 59 ⓦ www.bortarsasag.hu ◷ 10.00–20.00 Mon–Fri, 10.00–18.00 Sat ⓜ Metro: Moszkva tér ⓘ See website for further locations

Litea Bookshop and Tea Room Serving coffee, tea and good reads, this shop stocks a wide range of Hungarian books, CDs, guides, maps and postcards. Ⓐ I. Hess András tér 4 Ⓣ (1) 375 6987 Ⓦ www.litea.hu Ⓛ 10.00–18.00 daily Ⓝ Bus: 16 to Castle Hill

Opal Art This upmarket glass shop favours contemporary and Art Nouveau designs. Ⓐ I. Hess András tér 4 Ⓛ 10.00–17.00 daily Ⓝ Bus: 16 to Castle Hill

TAKING A BREAK

Café Gusto £ ❶ Serves great coffees, light salads and filling Hungarian specialities in this tucked-away spot near Margit híd (Margaret Bridge).

Pick out a special bottle to take home

I. Frankel Leó utca 12 (1) 316 3970 10.00–22.00 Mon–Sat
Tram: 4, 6, 17 to Margit híd

Miró Café £ ❷ A perfect stop for coffee and light snacks on quirky Úri utca, boasting an interior inspired by the works of Catalan artist Joan Miró. I. Úri utca 30 (1) 225 8125 09.00–24.00 daily

There are plenty of cosy coffee houses in Buda

Ruszwurm £ ❸ Made famous not only for its great cakes served since 1827 but also for its warm European styling, with finely crafted period furniture. ⓐ I. Szentháromság utca 7, off Úri utca ⓣ (1) 375 5284 ◷ 09.00–20.00 daily

Soho Café £ ❹ A lovely location for a cuppa. ⓐ I. Fő utca 25 (Buda side) ⓣ (1) 201 3807 ◷ 08.00–21.00 Mon–Fri, 09.00–21.00 Sat & Sun Ⓢ Metro: Batthyáni tér

AFTER DARK

Buda is known for its upmarket dining establishments located on leafy side streets with exquisite views. For a livelier bar-and-club scene, you'll need to cross the Danube.

RESTAURANTS

Náncsi Néni £ ❺ 'Aunt Nancy's' offers great Hungarian home cooking and live accordion music. A must to book ahead. ⓐ II. Ördögárok utca 80 ⓣ (1) 397 2742 ⓦ www.nancsineni.hu ◷ 12.00–23.00 Mon–Fri, 09.00–23.00 Sat & Sun Ⓢ Tram: 61 to Hűvösvölgy

Aranyszarvas ££ ❻ If you're game for game, this is the place for you. ⓐ I. Szarvas tér 1 ⓣ (1) 375 6451 ◷ 12.00–23.00 daily

Carne di Hall ££ ❼ This meat-eater's paradise also features an excellent selection of wines. ⓐ I. Bem rakpart 20, off Fő utca (Buda side) ⓣ (1) 201 8137 ◷ 12.00–24.00 daily Ⓢ Metro: Batthyány tér

Hyppolit ££ ❽ Retro neighbourhood eatery providing superb Hungarian dishes, all served with a smile. The terrace is lovely on summer days. ⓐ I. Attila útca 125 ⓣ (1) 201 7707 ⓛ 12.00–24.00 daily ⓝ Metro: Moszkva tér

Kéhli Vendéglő ££ ❾ Trek north a little into Óbuda for what locals swear is the best cooking in Budapest. Gypsy bands add atmosphere aplenty and the menu includes the likes of bone-marrow hotpot. ⓐ III. Mókus útca 22 ⓣ (1) 250 4241 ⓦ www.kehli.hu ⓛ 12.00–24.00 daily ⓝ Tram: 1 to Flórián tér

Malomtó ££ ❿ Asian-inspired flavours close to the Lukács Baths. Sit on the lakeside terrace if you can. ⓐ II. Frankel Leó utca 48 ⓣ (1) 336 1830 ⓛ 12.00–24.00 Tues–Sun ⓝ Tram: 17 to Lukács fürdő

Arany Kaviár £££ ⓫ Russian cuisine at its finest. ⓐ I. Ostrom utca 19 ⓣ (1) 201 6737 ⓛ 12.00–24.00 daily ⓝ Metro: Moszkva tér

Café Erté £££ ⓬ Continental haute cuisine at the foot of the Buda Hills. Delicious food complemented by excellent wines. ⓐ III. Alkotás útca 47 ⓣ (1) 225 3991 ⓦ www.cafeerte.hu ⓛ 12.00–15.00, 18.00–23.00 Mon–Sat ⓝ Tram: 59, 61 to Királyhago útca/tér

Csalogány 26 £££ ⓭ Seasonal, local ingredients are artfully converted into light Hungarian dishes. Reservations recommended. ⓐ I. Csalogány 26 ⓣ (1) 201 7892 ⓦ www.csalogany26.hu ⓛ 12.00–15.00 & 19.00–22.00 Tues–Sat ⓝ Metro: Moszkva tér

Fuji Japanese Restaurant £££ ⓮ For a landlocked country, the sushi is surprisingly good and the views from Rózsadomb are sublime. ⓐ II. Csatárka utca 54 ⓣ (1) 325 7111 ⓦ www.fujirestaurant.hu ⓛ 12.00–23.00 daily ⓝ Bus: 29, 111 to Zöldkert út

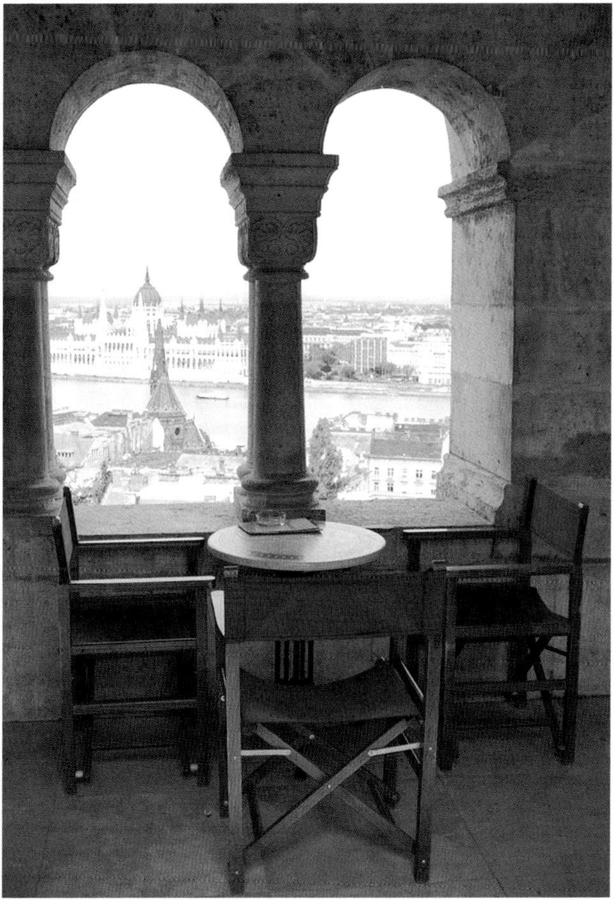

Some Buda restaurants offer fabulous views across the city

Floodlit Buda Castle towers over the Danube

Rivalda Restaurant £££ ⓯ Modern fusion Hungarian presented with impeccable service and wonderful vistas. Reservations recommended. ⓐ I. Színház utca 5–9, off Úri utca ⓣ (1) 489 0236 ⓑ 11.30–23.30 daily

BARS & CLUBS

A38 A moored Ukrainian party barge, featuring three floors to suit different tastes. Fab bands play on the lower deck; the middle deck offers a chilled-out restaurant and bar; the top deck grooves to excellent dance tunes. ⓐ XI. Pázmány Péter rakpart ⓣ (1) 464 3940 ⓦ www.a38.hu ⓑ 12.00–04.00 daily ⓒ Tram: 4, 6 to Petőfi híd or 2, 4, 6 to Boráros tér, then cross the bridge

Kaméleon Klub This club in the Mammut shopping centre stomps Buda with Latin and jazz beats until dawn. The crowd is an unpretentious mix of locals and expats, the interior is kitschedelic, and you can't help but have a great time. ⓐ II. Lövőház utca 1–5 ⓣ (1) 345 8547 ⓑ 20.00–05.00 daily ⓒ Metro: Moszkva tér

Libella Not far from Szent Gellért tér is a homely oasis serving some of the best beer in Buda. In the late hours, a mix of geeky engineering students, old diehards playing cards and sports fans watching the TV makes for an intriguing night out. ⓐ XI. Budafoki út 7 ⓣ (1) 209 4761 ⓑ 08.00–01.00 Mon–Fri, 12.00–01.00 Sat & Sun ⓒ Tram: 18, 19, 41, 47, 49 to Szent Gellért tér

Moszkva tér Bisztro Sitting pretty above the throng that is Moszkva tér metro station is this casual but hip bistro that reaches the pinnacle of cool in the summer sun. ⓐ II. Moszva tér ⓑ 12.00–24.00 Mon–Thur & Sun, 12.00–03.00 Fri & Sat

Pest: around Parliament

Pest is the true heart of the city, where people go about their daily lives. While the other side of the Danube was getting richer in the 19th century, factory workers, builders, shopkeepers and their families set up shop in Pest, making this a wholly Magyar metropolis. It quickly flourished, setting the stage for even greater expansion of Hungarian cultural pursuits, further stirring the stew that would lead to revolution.

At the end of the 19th century, Budapest's burgeoning population got down to business, making Budapest a world city. Nowhere is this more apparent than around the Parliament building, where grand boulevards, large squares and triumphant architecture house cultural treasures, high-end hotels and some of the best restaurants in Budapest.

Pest has seen some of the worst atrocities of the 20th century, and though the bullet holes are still visible in many façades, the municipality is committed to cleaning up the city with more green spaces and less traffic. The scars can stay. Hungarians prefer not to forget.

SIGHTS & ATTRACTIONS

Kossuth Lajos tér (Lajos Kossuth Square)

Named after the man who led the 1848–9 uprising against the Habsburgs, this square has splendid monuments paying tribute to Hungarian revolts against Austrian and later Soviet oppression. Metro: Kossuth Lajos tér

Nagy Imre-Szobor (Statue of Imre Nagy)

A statue has been erected in honour of the former prime minister who spearheaded the failed Hungarian Revolution of 1956. Imre Nagy, who was executed in 1958 (together with fellow leader Pal

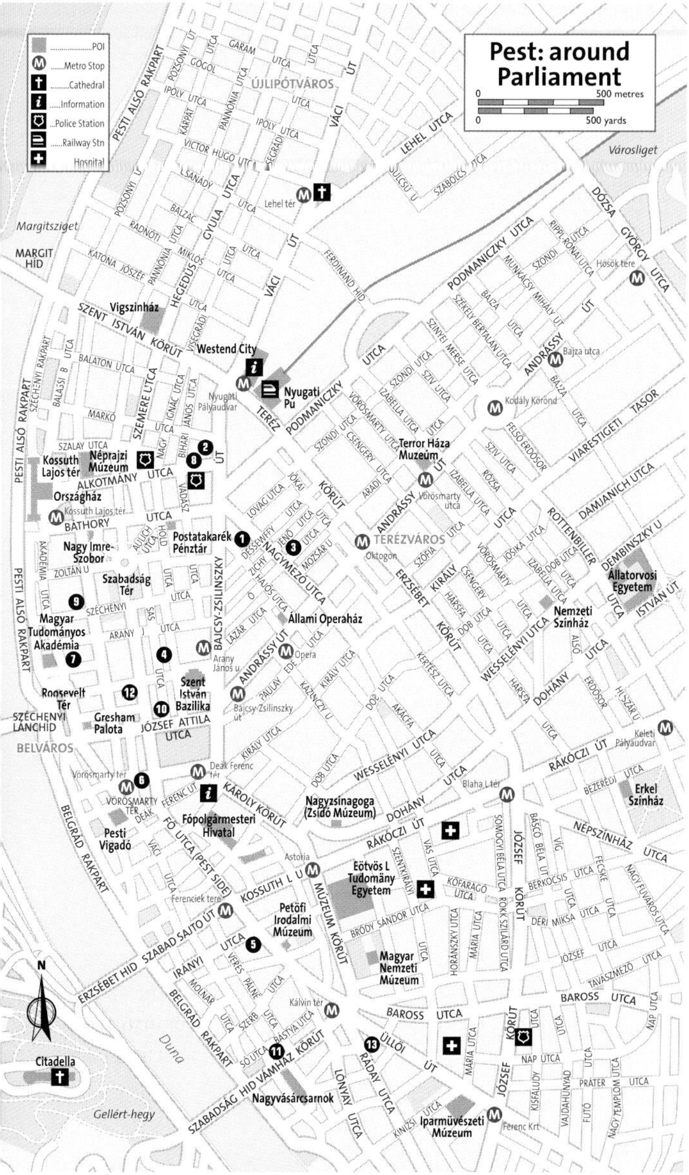

Pest: around Parliament
0 500 metres
0 500 yards
POI
Metro Stop
Cathedral
Information
Police Station
Railway Stn
Hospital
ÚJLIPÓTVÁROS
Városliget
Margitsziget
MARGIT HÍD
PESTI ALSÓ RAKPART
POZSONYI ÚT
GARAM
GOGOL
UTCA
IPOLY UTCA
KÁRPÁT
PANNONIA UTCA
VÁCI ÚT
LEHEL UTCA
VICTOR HUGO UTCA
SEGÉDI
SZABOLCS UTCA
DÓZSA GYÖRGY UTCA
Lehel tér
RADNÓTI
BALZAC
MIKLÓS
GYULA UTCA
HEGEDÜS
KATONA JÓZSEF
FERDINAND HÍD
PODMANICZKY UTCA
RIPPL-RÓNAI UTCA
SZONDI
MUNKÁCSY MIHÁLY UT
Hősök tere
Vigszínház
SZENT ISTVÁN KÖRÚT
VISEGRÁDI
Westend City
BALATON UTCA
SZÉCHENYI RAKPART
BALASSI B
SZEMERE UTCA
IGNÁC UTCA
JÁNOS UTCA
MARKÓ
Nyugati Pályaudvar
Nyugati Pu
TERÉZ
PODMANICZKY
VÖRÖSMARTY UTCA
IZABELLA UTCA
SZINYEI MERSE UTCA
SZÉKELY BERTALAN UTCA
BAJZA
ANDRÁSSY ÚT
Bajza utca
Kodály Körönd
VIARESTIGETI TASOR
FELSŐ ERDŐSOR
SZALAY UTCA
Kossuth Lajos tér
Néprajzi Múzeum
ALKOTMÁNY UTCA
NAGY
BIHARI
VADÁSZ
Országház
Kossuth Lajos tér
BÁTHORY UTCA
AULICH
HOLD
Postatakarék Pénztár
Terror Háza Múzeum
Vörösmarty utca
LOVAG UTCA
JÓKAI
KÖRÚT
ARADI
CSENGERY
SZONDI UTCA
RÓZSA
DAMJANICH UTCA
ROTTENBILLER
DEMBINSZKY U
Nagy Imre-Szobor
AKADÉMIA UTCA
ZOLTÁN U
DESSEWFFY
JENŐ
NAGYMEZŐ UTCA
MOZSÁR U
TERÉZVÁROS
Oktogon
ERZSÉBET KÖRÚT
KIRÁLY
SZÓFIA
HÁRSFA
DOB UTCA
JÓSIKA UTCA
Állatorvosi Egyetem
ISTVÁN ÚT
Szabadság Tér
SZÉCHENYI
SAS
BAJCSY-ZSILINSZKY
ZICHY
HAJÓS UTCA
Állami Operaház
Nemzeti Színház
WESSELÉNYI UTCA
Magyar Tudományos Akadémia
ARANY J
LÁZÁR UTCA
ANDRÁSSY ÚT
Opera
Arany János u
KERTÉSZ UTCA
Szent István Bazilika
PAULAY EDE
KAZINCZY U
DOB UTCA
AKÁCFA
DOHÁNY
ERDŐSOR
HUSZÁR U
Roosevelt Tér
SZÉCHENYI LÁNCHÍD
Gresham Palota
JÓZSEF ATTILA UTCA
Bajcsy-Zsilinszky út
KIRÁLY UTCA
Keleti Pályaudvar
RÁKÓCZI ÚT
BELVÁROS
Vörösmarty tér
Deák Ferenc tér
FERENC UT
KÁROLY KÖRÚT
Blaha L tér
BEZERÉDJ UTCA
Erkel Színház
VÖRÖSMARTY TÉR
DEÁK
Fópolgármesteri Hivatal
Nagyzsinagóga (Zsidó Múzeum)
SOMOGYI BÉLA UTCA
BACSÓ BÉLA ÚT
VÍG
NÉPSZÍNHÁZ UTCA
Pesti Vigadó
BELGRÁD RAKPART
VÁCI
FŐ UTCA (PEST SIDE)
Astoria
Eötvös L Tudomány Egyetem
SZENTKIRÁLYI
VAS UTCA
KŐFARAGÓ UTCA
JÓZSEF KÖRÚT
BERKOCSIS UTCA
FECSKE
NAGY FUVAROS UTCA
Ferenciek tere
KOSSUTH L U
MÚZEUM KÖRÚT
Petőfi Irodalmi Múzeum
BRÓDY SÁNDOR UTCA
HORÁNSZKY UTCA
MÁRIA UTCA
RÖKK SZILÁRD UTCA
DÉRI MIKSA UTCA
SZABAD SAJTÓ ÚT
ERZSÉBET HÍD
IRÁNYI
VERES PÁLNÉ
MOLNÁR
Magyar Nemzeti Múzeum
JÓZSEF UTCA
TAVASZMEZŐ UTCA
BAROSS UTCA
NAP UTCA
Kálvin tér
SZERB
BÁSTYA UTCA
Duna
ÜLLŐI ÚT
RÁDAY UTCA
SÓ UTCA
VÁMHÁZ KÖRÚT
Citadella
LÓNYAY UTCA
PRÁTER UTCA
KISFALUDY
VAJDAHUNYAD
FUTÓ
NAGY TEMPLOM UTCA
SZABADSÁG HÍD
Nagyvásárcsarnok
Gellért-hegy
KINIZSI UTCA
Iparművészeti Múzeum
Ferenc Krt
N

The Houses of Parliament stretch elegantly along the Danube

Maléter), has been enshrined in a life-size bronze statue to sit contemplating the parliament building – and democracy – for ever more. V. Vértanúk tere Metro: Kossuth Lajos tér

Országház (Houses of Parliament)
White neo-Gothic turrets and arches inspired by the Palace of Westminster stretch magnificently along the Danube. Inside, the impressive decoration, rich in Hungarian touches, winds its way down 20 km (12½ miles) of corridors. Take a quick 20- to 30-minute tour of the chambers when Parliament is not in session, and sit on the members' benches. Also on view is the holy crown, given to St Stephen by the pope in AD 1000 to commemorate Hungary's official inclusion in the Christian faith. The 2006 demonstrations took place on the grassed area in front of the building; it's here that protestors against Soviet occupation were shot in 1956, sparking the revolution.

ⓐ V. Kossuth Lajos tér ⓣ (1) 441 4415 ⓛ 10.00–18.00 Tues–Sun
ⓜ Metro: Kossuth Lajos tér

Postatakarék Pénztár (Postal Savings Bank)

Designed in 1901 by Ödön Lechner, Hungary's answer to Gaudí, this former postal savings bank is a stunning example of Art Nouveau architecture. Tours of the inside of the building are given only once a year, in May. ⓐ V. Hold utca 4 ⓣ (1) 428 2600 ⓜ Metro: Arany János utca

Roosevelt tér (Roosevelt Square)

At the head of the Lánchíd (Chain Bridge), this square's name has changed from 'Unloading Square' and 'Franz Josef's Square' to the current 'Roosevelt Square'. From the look of the hotels nearby, it could easily change its name again to 'Ritz Square'. ⓜ Metro: Kossuth Lajos tér

Szabadság tér (Liberty Square)

Laid out in 1886 on the site of an Austrian soldiers' barracks, this square has long been a symbol of Hungary's struggle for independence. The Soviet war memorial that stands here is one of the few remaining works of socialist art left in Budapest. A new 'intelligent' fountain livens up proceedings at the square's southern end. ⓜ Metro: Kossuth Lajos tér

CULTURE

Állami Operaház (State Opera House)

Designed by Miklós Ybl, the same architect who worked on St Stephen's Basilica (see page 84), this building is one of the finest historical buildings in town. Its walls feature 16 of the world's greatest composers, including Monteverdi, Mozart, Beethoven, Verdi, Bizet and Tchaikovsky.

The magnificent State Opera House

Inside, more than 7 kg (15 lb) of gold was used to decorate the horseshoe-shaped auditorium, which seats over 1,200 people. This venue features performances of ballet, classical music and opera nearly every day of the week. Even if you're not artistically inclined, just have a look at its amazing interior, and you may be persuaded to stay for a show. VI. Andrássy út 22 (1) 353 0170 & for guided tours (1) 332 8197 www.opera.hu Box office 10.00–19.00. Guided tours 15.00 & 16.00 Metro: Opera Admission charge

Gresham Palota (Gresham Palace)

John Gresham never set foot in Budapest. This building was commissioned 300 years after his death in 1904 by the Gresham Life

Assurance Company of London. If he had still been alive, he would surely have been pleased with the results. After its completion in 1906, it was the most cutting-edge building of the time, fitted out with all the latest amenities, including a unique central vacuum system. Though damaged in both World War II and the 1956 Revolution, the beautiful wrought-iron peacock entrance gates survived intact. Now, it is part of the Four Seasons Hotel chain, and houses a wonderful coffee house where you can ponder its history in style. ⓐ V. Roosevelt tér 6 ⓣ (1) 268 6000 ⓦ www.fourseasons.com ⓛ Variable: phone to arrange a visit ⓜ Metro: Vörösmarty tér

Néprajzi Múzeum (Ethnographic Museum)
The grand location opposite Parliament makes it safe to assume that Hungarians take their culture seriously. A huge entrance hall, with chandeliers and marble staircases, leads to colourfully exhibited costumes, toys, objects associated with weddings and funerals, and depictions of village and farm life, all explained in English. ⓐ V. Kossuth Lajos tér 12 ⓣ (1) 473 2400 ⓦ www.neprajz.hu ⓛ 10.00–18.00 Tues–Sun ⓜ Metro: Kossuth Lajos tér ⓘ Admission charge

RETAIL THERAPY

It's an expensive undertaking to shop in this district, filled with quality antique items and one-of-a-kind finds. If you're looking for that special something, this may be the place for you.

Bestsellers Home from home for expats, offering the best in English-language literature. ⓐ V. Október 6 utca 11 ⓣ (1) 312 1295 ⓦ www.bestsellers.hu ⓛ 09.00–18.30 Mon–Fri, 10.00–17.00 Sat, 10.00–16.00 Sun ⓜ Metro: Arany János utca

SZENT ISTVÁN BAZILIKA (ST STEPHEN'S BASILICA)
St Stephen's Basilica is a must-see for any visitor. It's perfect now, but hasn't always been. After the original dome fell in 1868, Hungarian architect Miklós Ybl, who had only recently taken over the project, set to work repairing his architectural predecessor's mistakes. Although it suffered damage from bombings in World War II, the church has remained standing thanks to Ybl's sounder neo-Renaissance design. In the Szent jobb kápolna (Chapel of the Sacred Right) lies Catholic Hungary's most revered and creepy relic – what is claimed to be the mummified right hand of St Stephen. Extra lighting has been added to the nave for appreciating all the works of art and sculptures, and the organ has been completely renovated. ⓐ V. Szent István tér 1 ⓣ (1) 317 2859 ⓦ www.bazilika.biz ◷ 09.00–17.00 daily ⓝ Metro: Arany János utca or Bajcsy-Zsilinszky út

Bolt Unique and supremely wearable clothes and accessories, and furnishings too – all by Hungarian designers. ⓐ VII. Kertész útca 42–44 ⓣ (1) 381 9051 ⓦ www.boltmuhely.hu ◷ 11.00–19.00 Mon–Fri, 11.00–15.00 Sat ⓝ Metro: Oktogon

Eclectick Design Shop A respite from the usual high-street designs, this is the place to pick up funky Hungarian threads. ⓐ V. Irányi utca 20 ⓣ (1) 266 3341 ⓦ www.eclectick.hu ◷ 10.00–19.00 Mon–Fri, 11.00–16.00 Sat ⓝ Metro: Ferenciek tere

Orlando Collection Haute couture meets the street in wonderful prêt-à-porter by young Hungarian designers. ⓐ V. Zoltán utca 11

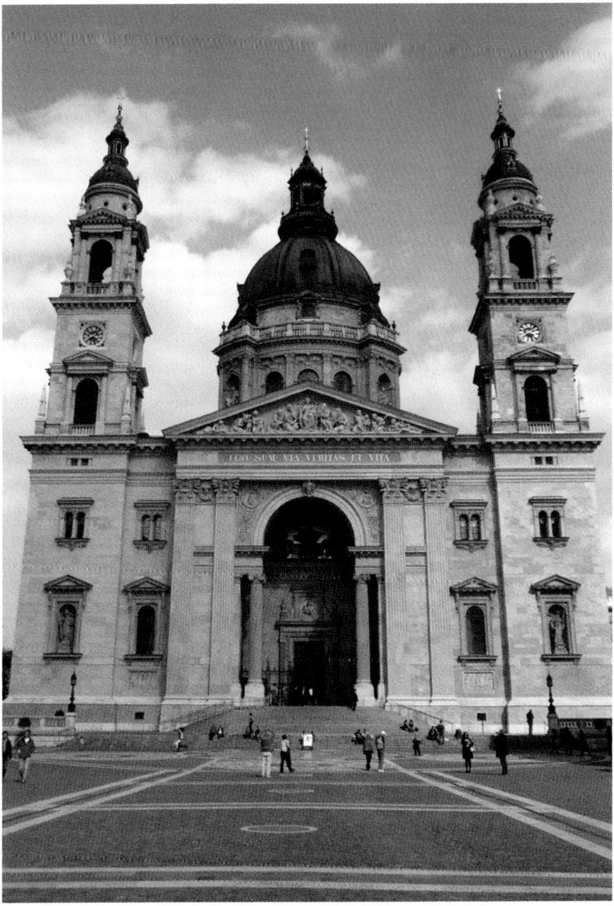

St Stephen's Basilica is Budapest's largest church

ⓣ 20 938 6528 (mobile) ⓦ www.orlandocollection.hu ⓛ 10.00–18.00 Mon–Fri, 10.00–13.00 Sat ⓜ Metro: Kossuth Lajos tér

Pintér Antik Housed in what used to be an air-raid shelter, this large, flaunty antiques shop serves coffee as well. ⓐ V. Falk Miksa utca 10 ⓣ (1) 311 3030 ⓦ www.pinterantik.hu ⓛ 10.00–18.00 Mon–Fri, 10.00–14.00 Sat ⓜ Metro: Kossuth Lajos tér

Vasseva Clothing, bedding and accessories with a thoroughly modern and minimalist touch. ⓐ VI. Paulay Ede utca 67 ⓣ (1) 342 8159 ⓛ 12.00–20.00 Mon–Fri ⓜ Metro: Opera

Virág Judit Galéria és Aukciósház An excellent collection of antique paintings and porcelain for sale. ⓐ V. Falk Miksa utca 30 ⓣ (1) 312 2071 ⓛ 10.00–18.00 Mon–Fri, 10.00–13.00 Sat ⓜ Metro: Kossuth Lajos tér

Westend City Center This shopping centre, polished, pristine and usually packed with people, features more than 400 upmarket shops, cinemas, amusement arcades and even a sightseeing balloon. You won't find any unusual bargains here, but you may find some fun, especially when the temperatures soar or the weather is uncooperative. ⓐ VI. Váci ut 1–3 ⓣ (1) 238 7777 ⓦ www.westend.hu ⓛ 08.00–23.00 Mon–Sat, 08.00–22.00 Sun ⓜ Metro: Nyugati pu

TAKING A BREAK

Balett Cipő £ ❶ 'Ballet Shoes' café has a great atmosphere and will keep you on your toes, with a long list of coffees, cocktails and even some salads. ⓐ VI. Hajós utca 14 ⓣ (1) 269 3114 ◷ 10.00–24.00 daily ⓝ Metro: Opera

Beckett's £ ❷ The friendly, informal centre of Budapest's expat scene. It certainly serves great pub grub, plus there's Guinness on tap and live music. ⓐ V. Bajcsy-Zsilinszky út 72 ⓣ (1) 311 1035 ⓦ www.becketts.hu ◷ 12.00–01.00 Mon–Fri & Sun, 12.00–02.00 Sat ⓝ Metro: Nyugati pu

Café Bouchon £ ❸ A popular restaurant serving international dishes in an unpretentious setting – get there early for a seat. ⓐ VI. Zichy Jenő utca 33 ⓣ (1) 353 4094 ⓦ www.cafebouchon.hu ◷ 09.00–23.00 Mon–Sat ⓝ Metro: Oktogon

Café Kör £ ❹ Sample excellent national cuisine in this cosy Hungarian eatery with an appropriate-sounding name! ⓐ V. Sas utca 17 ⓣ (1) 311 0053 ◷ 10.00–22.00 Mon–Sat ⓝ Metro: Arany János utca

Centrál Kávéház £ ❺ This place has reinvented itself, but remains an old-fashioned watering hole for intellectuals, travellers and Budapesters in the know. Also serves excellent meals at a reasonable price. ⓐ V. Károlyi Mihály utca 9 ⓣ (1) 266 2110 ⓦ www.centralkavehaz.hu ◷ 08.00–24.00 daily ⓝ Metro: Ferenciek tere

Gerbeaud £ ❻ The place to get fuelled on gooey Hungarian and Viennese sweets and hot chocolate that's literally just melted milk chocolate. The interior is lovely but unfortunately the service sometimes isn't. Try your luck. ⓐ V. Vörösmarty tér 7 ⓣ (1) 429 9000 ◷ 09.00–21.00 daily ⓝ Metro: Vörösmarty tér

AFTER DARK

RESTAURANTS

Govinda £ ❼ Simple veggie Indian-style offerings. ⓐ V. Vigyázó Ferenc utca 4, off Akadémia 6 utca ⓣ (1) 269 1625 ⓛ 12.00–21.00 daily ⓝ Metro: Arany János utca

Hummus £ ❽ Simple but expertly executed hummus, salad and falafel. ⓐ V. Alkotmány útca 20 ⓣ (1) 302 1385 ⓦ www.hummusbar.hu ⓛ 10.00–22.00 Mon–Fri, 12.00–22.00 Sat & Sun ⓝ Metro: Nyugati pu

Momotaro Ramen £ ❾ A tasty mixture of Chinese and Japanese. You won't linger, as the seating isn't too comfortable, but you will leave happy and full. ⓐ V. Széchenyi utca 16 ⓣ (1) 269 3802 ⓛ 11.00–22.00 daily ⓝ Metro: Kossuth Lajos tér

Dió Restaurant ££ ❿ Trendy contemporary Hungarian food. ⓐ V. Sas utca 4 ⓣ (1) 328 0360 ⓛ 12.00–24.00 daily ⓝ Metro: Arany János utca

Pampas Argentine Steak House ££ ⓫ Succulent imported prime Angus steak. ⓐ V. Vámház körút 6 ⓣ (1) 411 1750 ⓦ www.steak.hu ⓛ 12.00–02.00 daily ⓝ Metro: Kálvín tér

Tom George Italiano ££ ⓬ Great pizzas, grilled meat and fish. ⓐ V. Október 6 utca 8 ⓣ (1) 266 3525 ⓛ 12.00–24.00 Mon–Thur & Sun, 12.00–01.00 Fri & Sat ⓝ Metro: Vörösmarty tér

Costes £££ ⓭ Hungary's first Michelin-starred restaurant. Sample the incredible tasting menu or select seasonal mains. Reservations are a must. IX. Raday utca 4 (1) 219 0696 www.costes.hu 12.00–15.30, 18.30–24.00 Wed–Sun Metro: Kálvin tér

BARS & CLUBS

Columbus Pub & Jazz Club This moored party boat is part restaurant, part club and hosts lively jazz gigs from 20.00 nightly. V. Vigadó tér 4 (1) 266 9013 www.columbuspub.hu 12.00–24.00 daily Metro: Vörösmarty tér

Fat Mo's An American-style basement bar with great bands and great steaks. V. Nyáry Pál utca 11 (1) 267 3199 www.fatmo.hu 12.00–02.00 Mon–Wed, 12.00–04.00 Thur & Fri, 18.00–04.00 Sat, 18.00–02.00 Sun Metro: Kálvin tér

Gödör Klub Meaning 'pit', this subterranean gem (with terraces) boasts food, drink and culture for an eclectic crowd. V. Erzsébet tér 20 201 3868 (mobile) www.godorklub.hu 10.00–late daily Metro: Deák Ferenc tér

Pótkulcs A sprawling collection of rooms for late-night revelry. VI. Csengery útca 65b (1) 269 1050 www.potkulcs.hu 17.00–01.30 Sun–Wed, 17.00–02.30 Thur–Sat Metro: Nyugati pu

Trafó Bár Tangó Contemporary art venue with a bar and club space for bright young Budapesters. IX. Liliom utca 41 (1) 456 2040 www.trafo.hu 18.00–04.00 daily Metro: Ferenc körút

Tulipán Presszó A bar that never sleeps, so bring a pack of cards and join the insomniac locals and tourists. V. Nádor utca 34 (1) 269 5043 24 hours Metro: Kossuth Lajos tér

Central Pest & the Városliget

In Budapest, all roads lead to Váci utca and Fő utca. It's no wonder: the former was historically the main road to the city; the latter is the result of a recent EU/Hungarian jointly funded project. Now a pedestrian-only thoroughfare on the Pest side of the river, it is filled with chic cafés, upmarket boutiques and speciality shops. Window-shopping and people-watching are the favoured activities, and sitting at an outdoor café, enjoying the flow of locals and tourists alike, is one of the primary pleasures.

Northeast is Pest's most beautiful street, Andrássy út, where you'll encounter more of what makes this city wonderful: its commitment to making movement pleasurable. You will follow rows of apartment buildings, walk past theatres and reach a leafy diplomatic quarter, where the boulevards become quieter and more picturesque. Running just beneath the street is the Metró, the first underground line in continental Europe. When you make your way to the Városliget (City Park, see page 93), the space and fresh air will intoxicate you.

At night, kick up your heels or let off some steam in one of the many cafés, clubs and bars that surround Liszt Ferenc tér (Franz Liszt Square), close to the Oktogon metro station for a ride home afterwards.

For a wonderfully unique evening out, keep an eye out for posters scattered around Pest with the word '*kert*' scribbled on. This literally translates into 'garden', but *kerts* in a socialising sense are essentially bars squatting in old buildings that may or may not be crumbling around your ears. Locals young and old will hang out in these *kerts*, where the drinks are cheap and food is often simple soups or rolls. Unfortunately, some of these *kerts* shut down during the winter months and may or may not open up in the same spot, meaning you have to rediscover your favourite drinking hole when

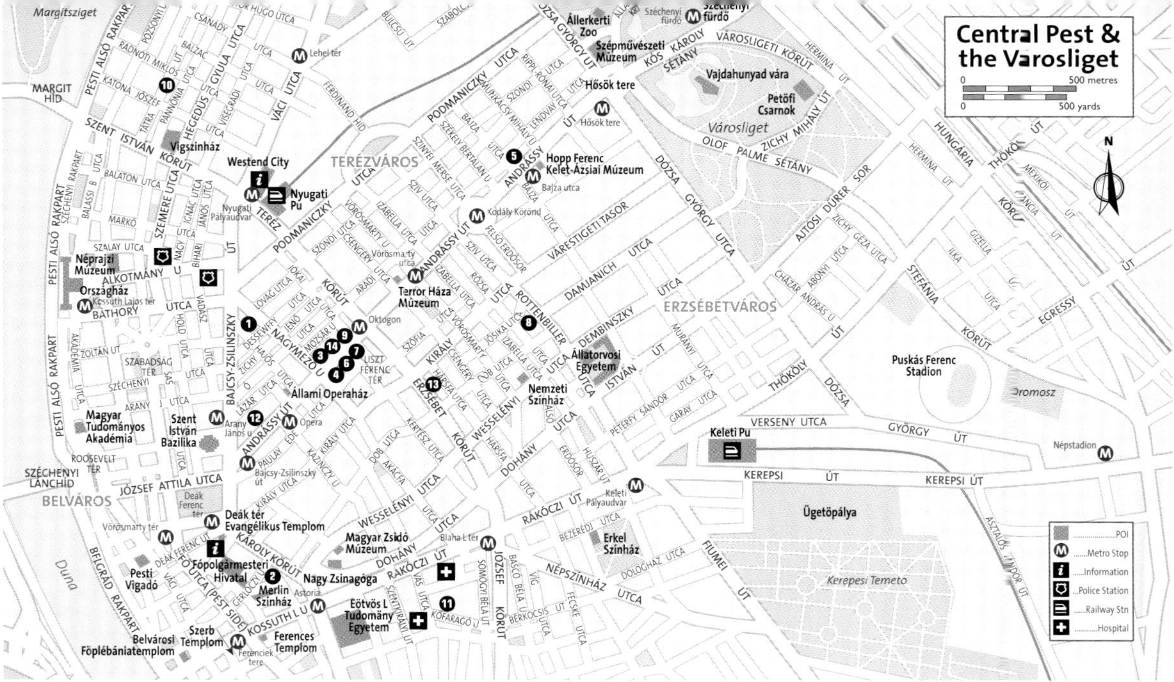

Central Pest & the Varosliget
0 500 metres
0 500 yards
N
POI
Metro Stop
Information
Police Station
Railway Stn
Hospital
Margitsziget
MARGIT HÍD
Duna
SZÉCHENYI LÁNCHÍD
BELVÁROS
TERÉZVÁROS
ERZSÉBETVÁROS
Városliget
Állerkerti Zoo
Szépművészeti Múzeum
Széchenyi fürdő
Vajdahunyad vára
Petőfi Csarnok
Hősök tere
Hopp Ferenc Kelet-Ázsiai Múzeum
Bajza utca
Kodály Körönd
Lehel tér
Vígszínház
Westend City
Nyugati Pu
Nyugati Pályaudvar
Néprajzi Múzeum
Országház
Kossuth Lajos tér
Terror Háza Múzeum
Vörösmarty utca
Oktogon
Liszt Ferenc tér
Állami Operaház
Opera
Arany János u
Szent István Bazilika
Magyar Tudományos Akadémia
Bajcsy-Zsilinszky út
Deák Ferenc tér
Deák tér
Evangélikus Templom
Vörösmarty tér
Pesti Vigadó
Főpolgármesteri Hivatal
Merlin Színház
Nagy Zsinagóga
Magyar Zsidó Múzeum
Astoria
Eötvös L Tudomány Egyetem
Ferences Templom
Ferenciek tere
Szerb Templom
Belvárosi Főplébániatemplom
Állatorvosi Egyetem
Nemzeti Színház
Blaha L tér
Keleti Pályaudvar
Keleti Pu
Erkel Színház
Ügetőpálya
Kerepesi Temető
Puskás Ferenc Stadion
Népstadion
Dromosz
ANDRÁSSY ÚT
PODMANICZKY UTCA
DÓZSA GYÖRGY ÚT
VÁROSLIGETI KÖRÚT
OLOF PALME SÉTÁNY
ZICHY MIHÁLY ÚT
AJTÓSI DÜRER SOR
HUNGÁRIA KÖRÚT
THÖKÖLY ÚT
STEFÁNIA ÚT
VÁRESTIGETI TASOR
DAMJANICH UTCA
DEMBINSZKY UTCA
ROTTENBILLER UTCA
ISTVÁN ÚT
KEREPSI ÚT
VERSENY UTCA
FIUMEI ÚT
RÁKÓCZI ÚT
NÉPSZÍNHÁZ UTCA
JÓZSEF KÖRÚT
ERZSÉBET KÖRÚT
TERÉZ KÖRÚT
KIRÁLY UTCA
WESSELÉNYI UTCA
DOHÁNY UTCA
KÁROLY KÖRÚT
KOSSUTH L U
FŐ UTCA (PEST SIDE)
JÓZSEF ATTILA UTCA
BAJCSY-ZSILINSZKY ÚT
NAGYMEZŐ U
SZENT ISTVÁN KÖRÚT
HEGEDŰS GYULA UTCA
VÁCI UTCA
PESTI ALSÓ RAKPART
BELGRÁD RAKPART
SZEMERE UTCA
ALKOTMÁNY U
BÁTHORY UTCA
ASZTALOS SÁNDOR ÚT

the city thaws. An institution in the city is a *kert* called **Szimpla** (W www.szimpla.hu), and its website sums up *kert*dom beautifully.

SIGHTS & ATTRACTIONS

Belvárosi Főplébániatemplom (Inner City Parish Church)

This is the oldest building in Pest. Originally a 12th-century Romanesque church, it has survived the ravages of Mongols and Turks. In the 16th century it was converted into a mosque, and after World War II the church was again threatened, this time by the Hungarian authorities who planned to demolish it in order to rebuild Erzsébet híd (Elizabeth Bridge). As you can see, the bridge was skilfully re-routed around the church. Behind the high altar, you'll find an amazingly intact Turkish prayer niche. a V. Március 15. tér 2 t (1) 318 3108 08.00–19.00 daily Metro: Ferenciek tere

Deák tér Evangélikus Templom (Deák Square Lutheran Church)

Built in 1809, this building originally housed military uniforms. A couple of years later, it became a Protestant church. This building is typical in its Protestant lack of ornamentation, with a simple neoclassical design. The church can be seen during services (a V. Deák tér 5 10.00–18.00 Tues–Sun). It can also be seen as part of a visit to the next-door **National Lutheran Museum** (a V. Deák tér 4 t (1) 317 4173 W www.lutheran.hu 10.00–18.00 Tues–Sun Metro: Deák Ferenc tér).

Ferences Templom (Franciscan Church)

This 13th-century church was, like many of the other churches in Budapest, converted into a mosque during the Turkish occupation of the 16th and 17th centuries. Rebuilt by Franciscan monks in the late 18th century, the façade and Baroque altar are remarkable. V. Ferenciek tere 9 (1) 317 3322 07.00–19.00 daily Metro: Ferenciek tere

Hősök tere (Heroes' Square)

This square was once the place for anti-Communist demonstrations. Now its grand expanse and perfect glassy surface are appreciated by skateboarders and BMX stunt punters. The Millennium Monument here was erected in 1896 to commemorate the 1,000th anniversary of the Hungarians' settlement of the Carpathian Basin. Standing on top of a column is the Archangel Gabriel, who appeared to St Stephen in a dream and offered him the crown of Hungary. The 'seven chieftains' sit at the foot of the column, representing the seven Magyar tribes who settled in Hungary in the 9th century. Metro: Hősök tere

Szerb Templom (Serbian Church)

Built in the Baroque style by Serbian settlers in 1698, the church functions according to Greek Orthodox tradition: a wooden railing separates the women's and men's areas, and an iconostasis surrounds the gallery to keep all the churchgoers in line. V. Szerb utca 2–4 08.00–19.00 daily Metro: Ferenciek tere or Kálvin tér

Városliget (City Park)

Once unusable swampland, this is now Budapest's largest park, offering something for everyone. The most imposing building is Vajdahunyad vára (Vajdahunyad Castle), a hotchpotch of architectural styles (Romanesque, Gothic, Renaissance and Baroque) designed to represent more than 20 famous Hungarian buildings. The only area of the castle open to the public is the **Museum of Agriculture** ((1) 363 1973 10.00–16.00 daily), which has an interesting exhibition about Hungarian winemaking. In winter, the artificial lake turns into a vast skating rink. Other attractions in the Városliget include the Széchenyi Baths (see page 46). The **Petőfi Csarnok** (www.petoficsarnok.hu), a concert venue, is also located here. Metro: Hősök tere

CULTURE

Hopp Ferenc Kelet-Ázsiai Múzeum (Ferenc Hopp Museum of East Asian Art)

When Hungarian businessman Ferenc Hopp died in 1919, he left behind over 20,000 objects from India and the Far East. Ancient Buddhist art is shown alongside Japanese, Indian, Tibetan and Nepalese pieces. VI. Andrássy út 103 (1) 322 8476 www.hoppmuzeum.hu 10.00–16.00 Tues–Sun Metro: Bajza utca Admission charge (except national holidays)

Merlin Színház (Merlin Theatre)

This is the only theatre in Budapest that offers regular performances in English. Evocative performers make shows contemporary and thought-provoking. There's also a bar and a club for late-night happenings. V. Gerlóczy utca 4 (1) 317 9338 Metro: Astoria, Deák Ferenc tér or Ferenciek tere

Szépművészeti Múzeum (Museum of Fine Arts)

This museum houses an important collection of non-Hungarian art, with items dating from the Egyptian era to the present, and galleries that are home to famous works by El Greco, Goya, Rembrandt and Rubens. Exciting temporary exhibitions are also worth a visit. XIV. Hősök tere (1) 469 7100 www.szepmuveszeti.hu 10.30–17.30 Tues–Sun Metro: Hősök tere

The magnificent interior of Budapest's Great Synagogue

BUDAPEST'S JEWISH QUARTER

Forbidden to live within the city walls, Budapest's Jews traditionally occupied a quarter bordered by Andrássy út and Rákóczi út in the VII district. During the 1848 uprising, they stood against the Habsburgs with their fellow Budapesters. By 1867, they obtained legal equality, thereby attracting the immigration of Jews from surrounding countries. Jewish businesses boomed, which helped Budapest on its way to becoming a great financial centre, and by 1910 there were more than 200,000 of them in the city, making up nearly 25 per cent of its population. During the 1930s and 1940s, Budapest's Jews suffered pressure from right-wing government campaigns, followed by fascist ideologies that would wall them off into a ghetto within the capital. World War II saw the loss of some 700,000 Hungarian Jews, but the Budapest ghetto, established within the confines of the old Jewish quarter, was the only ghetto in Europe that wasn't completely destroyed. Here, the arrival of the Red Army really did mean liberation. Today, more than 3,000 Orthodox Jews live in the Jewish quarter, where you can find many Orthodox synagogues built in protest against the Great Synagogue, which some clerics argue is too close to Christianity for comfort. Besides synagogues, you'll find kosher markets, and get a feeling for Jewish neighbourhood life. The following will provide an enhanced understanding of this unforgettable part of the city:

Jewish Quarter Walking Tours Perfect to learn more about the Jewish tradition in Budapest. Tours leave from the

Great Synagogue (see below): choose from a 2½-hour tour that also takes in the synagogue, with an opportunity to eat kosher food along the way, and a 60-minute walk around the quarter. Ⓐ VII. Dohány utca 2 Ⓣ (1) 317 2754 Ⓦ www.greatsynagogue.hu Ⓛ Tours depart 10.30 & 13.30 Mon–Thur, 10.30 Fri, 11.30 Sun Ⓜ Metro: Astoria ⓘ Admission charge

Magyar Zsidó Múzeum (Hungarian Jewish Museum)
Established in 1931, this museum houses Jewish relics from the 18th and 19th centuries, from both Hungary and abroad, grouped according to religious significance. The exhibition ends with moving photo and press documentation of the insanity of the Holocaust in Hungary. The museum stands where Theodor Herzl (1860–1904), the father of Zionism, was born. Ⓐ VII. Dohány utca 2 Ⓣ (1) 343 6756 Ⓛ 10.00–17.00 Mon–Thur, 10.00–14.00 Fri & Sun Ⓜ Metro: Astoria

Nagy Zsinagóga (Great Synagogue) This synagogue is the second largest in the world. Completed in 1859, its onion domes and façades are Byzantine-inspired. The design also expresses 19th-century Hungarian Jews' aspirations to assimilate, with twin towers that look like church steeples, and an organ chamber. Germans turned the synagogue into a detention camp in World War II; more than 3,000 Jews who didn't survive were buried in mass graves in the courtyard. Ⓐ VII. Dohány utca 2 Ⓣ (1) 317 2754 Ⓦ www.greatsynagogue.hu Ⓛ 10.00–17.00 Mon–Thur, 10.00–14.00 Fri & Sun Ⓜ Metro: Astoria ⓘ Admission charge includes the Hungarian Jewish Museum next door (see above)

Terror Háza Múzeum (House of Terror Museum)
This controversial museum, built to commemorate the horrors that Hungary suffered under the two terror regimes of the Nazis and the Communists, opened its doors in 2002. For some, it's over the top; for others, a chilling reminder of what can happen if we get too complacent about world politics. The interrogation rooms, torture devices, propaganda samples and video clips of interviews with survivors from the 1956 Revolution bring the points home.
VI. Andrássy út 60 (1) 374 2600 www.terrorhaza.hu 10.00–18.00 daily Metro: Vörösmarty utca Admission charge

RETAIL THERAPY

Folkart Centrum This is the largest folk-art shop in Hungary and offers a wide range of authentically handcrafted products from all over the country. Clothing, embroidery, homespun wool, handwoven articles, painted Easter eggs, porcelain, pottery, traditional flasks, wooden carvings and other small souvenir items make perfect gifts. Váci utca 58 (1) 318 5840 www.folkartcentrum.hu 10.00–19.00 daily Metro: Ferenciek tere

Louis Vuitton Situated in a prime piece of real estate, this is the place to pick up your genuine Vuitton luggage. VI. Andrassy út 24 (1) 373 0487 10.00–19.00 Mon–Fri, 11.00–18.00 Sat Metro: Opera

Nagyvásárcsarnok (Great Market Hall) Situated on the Pest side of the Szabadság híd (Liberty Bridge), the Great Market Hall is a remarkable building that should not be missed, though the looming exterior is far more stunning that the cluttered interior (it was designed by

The controversial House of Terror Museum

Gustave Eiffel of Eiffel Tower fame). Make your way past tourists and grandmas buying ingredients for the evening goulash, and bask in the reality of it all. If reality becomes too much, in the basement a grocer sells all those things you miss from back home. IX. Vámház körút 1–3 (1) 217 6067 06.00–17.00 Mon–Fri, 06.00–14.00 Sat Metro: Kálvin tér

Párizsi udvar (Parisian Arcade) This sumptuous and elaborate arcade was completed in 1913, and originally housed the Inner City Savings Bank. It functions today as a shopping arcade, but is currently awaiting refurbishment. As you meander through the building, note the bee-inspired details (bees were a symbol of thrift) and the arched glass ceiling. V. Ferenciek tere 10–11 Metro: Ferenciek tere

VÁCI UTCA: SHOP TILL YOU DROP

It's impossible to count the number of shops lining Váci utca, in Budapest's premier shopping district. Suffice to say that once you're there, you've arrived in shoppers' heaven. A stroll around this spendthrift thoroughfare takes you past swish boutiques, jewellers, perfumeries and art galleries. Thankfully, it's not all expensive or out of bounds for the more budget-conscious traveller. Radiating from the hub of Váci utca are smaller, lesser-known streets presenting you with a rush of bookshops, cafés, gourmet wine shops and world-famous, oddly affordable confectioners. There's something for everyone. Párizsi utca has Szamos marzipan and ice cream; Fehérhajó utca sells healing minerals; the Csók Gallery on the corner of Pesti Barnabás utca sells works by modern Hungarian artists; and Kígyó utca is gradually turning into a street of fine Zsolnay porcelain, famous for its golds, greens and blues. The possibilities are endless, but you know your limit, and so does your credit-card company. Ⓜ Metro: Ferenciek tere

TAKING A BREAK

Chagall £ ❶ Great sandwiches served with Czech beer make a winning combination. ⓐ VI. Hajós utca 27 ⓣ (1) 302 4614 ⓛ 09.00–24.00 daily Ⓜ Metro: Opera or Arany János utca

Gerlóczy Káféház £ ❷ Fabulously elegant coffee shop with a wonderful restaurant attached. ⓐ V. Ker Gerlóczy útca ⓣ (1) 234 0953 ⓦ www.gerloczy.hu ⓛ 07.00–23.00 daily Ⓜ Metro: Astoria

Mai Manó Kávézó £ ❸ Arty, very arty. More Czech beer among the displays of black-and-white photos. A moody, smoky environment inside; outdoors perfect for an alfresco coffee. ⓐ VI. Nagymező utca 20 ⓣ (1) 269 5642 ◷ 10.00–01.00 daily Ⓜ Metro: Opera

Book Café ££ ❹ Revive in Art Nouveau splendour at the beautifully restored Párizsi Nagy Áruház. Coffee, a piano and a bookshop: what more could you want? ⓐ V. Andrassy utca 39 ◷ 10.00–20.00 daily Ⓜ Metro: Oktogon

Kogart ££ ❺ A gallery restaurant serving thoughtfully prepared dishes to meat-eaters and vegetarians alike. ⓐ VI. Andrássy út 112 ⓣ (1) 354 3820 ◷ 10.00–18.00 daily Ⓜ Metro: Bajza utca

Menza ££ ❻ Great food in a retro setting makes this spot popular with students and tourists alike. Try the *lángos*, a Hungarian speciality. ⓐ VI. Liszt Ferenc tér 2 ⓣ (1) 413 1482 ◷ 10.00–24.00 daily Ⓜ Metro: Oktogon

AFTER DARK

RESTAURANTS

Buena Vista £ ❼ Classy, with warm woods, and warmer Mediterranean flavours. The outdoor terrace is a must in the summer months. ⓐ VI. Liszt Ferenc tér 4–5 ⓣ (1) 344 6303 ◷ 11.00–24.00 daily Ⓜ Metro: Oktogon

Napfényes Ízek £ ❽ A fabulous vegetarian restaurant. ⓐ VII. Rózsa utca 39 ⓣ (1) 313 5555 ◷ 12.00–22.30 daily Ⓜ Metro: Vörösmarty útca

Alfresco dining in Franz Liszt Square

Cotton Club ££ 9 Chicago reinvented in Budapest with restaurant, smoking room, gambling den and live music. VI. Jókai utca 26 (1) 354 0886 www.cottonclub.hu 12.00–24.00 daily Metro: Oktogon

Firkász ££ 10 A place where writers meet, pianists play and waiters serve good old-fashioned food. XIII. Tátra utca 18 (1) 450 1118 www.firkaszetterem.hu 12.00–24.00 daily Tram: 2, 4, 6 to Jászai Mari tér

Fülemüle ££ 11 Tasty, classy, non-kosher Jewish dishes. VIII. Kőfaragó utca 5 (1) 266 7974 www.fulemule.hu 12.00–22.00 Sun–Thur, 12.00–23.00 Fri & Sat Metro: Blaha Lujza tér

Goa ££ ⓬ Arty surroundings and contemporary fusion cuisine ranging from Asian to Italian. VI. Andrássy út 8 (1) 302 2570 www.goaworld.hu 12.00–24.00 daily Metro: Bajcsy-Zsilinszky utca

Bock Bisztro £££ ⓭ Superb Hungarian cuisine lovingly prepared to complement master vintner József Bock's wines. VII. Corinthia Grand Hotel Royal, Erzsébet körút 43–49 (1) 321 0340 www.bockbisztro.hu 12.00–24.00 daily Metro: Oktogon

Klassz £££ ⓮ A very trendy and rather expensive restaurant – so exclusive, you can't even book a table. VI. Andrássy út 41 11.30–23.00 Mon–Sat, 11.30–18.30 Sun Metro: Arany János utca

BARS & CLUBS

Champs Sport Pub Missing your football team? Champs has booths with private televisions. VII. Dohány utca 20 (1) 413 1655 www.champs.hu 11.00–02.00 daily Metro: Blaha Lujza tér

Old Man's Music Club This is the place in Budapest to catch the blues. VII. Akácfa utca 13 (1) 322 7645 www.oldmans.hu 15.00–04.00 daily Metro: Blaha Lujza tér

Szóda Café A laid-back bar with illustrations and original graphics adorning the walls and ceiling. VII. Wesselényi utca 18 (1) 461 0007 www.szoda.com 09.00–06.00 daily Metro: Astoria

Vittula This expat-owned club is a charming if smoky spot known for playing great tunes. VIII. Kertész útca 4 www.vittula.hu 18.00–02.00 Mon–Wed & Sun, 18.00–04.00 Thur–Sat Metro: Blaha Lujza tér

Around Budapest

Though the city centre has enough to keep anyone busy for a lifetime, Budapest is quickly sprawling out of its city limits, reaching towards its ancient historical roots in Aquincum, or its prehistory in the caves of the Buda Hills, blurring the distinction between town and suburb. Places that once had to be considered a full day trip have now been connected by the HÉV, the suburban rail network that links central Budapest with greater Budapest. The outer reaches of the city are also now well served by frequent and convenient bus services.

If you want to get your shoulders tanned in rugged nature or breathe the air of Budapest's history, you should take at least one quick jaunt to some of these sites. They're worth the effort, and you'll make it back in time to dance on a few more tables before your flight home.

SIGHTS & ATTRACTIONS

Aquincum Roman ruins

In the 2nd and 3rd centuries AD, Aquincum was the bustling capital of the Roman province Pannonia, serving as a trading settlement and garrison town. The excavated ruins give us a glimpse into public and private life at the time. Highlights of the museum are a reconstructed 3rd-century water organ, temporary exhibitions, chronoscopes showing the original appearance of buildings, and the small amphitheatre right next door. Ironically, the ruins sit among the suburban sprawl of Budapest. ⓐ III. Szentendrei út 139 ⓦ www.aquincum.hu ⓑ 09.00–18.00 Tues–Sun (May–Sept); 10.00–16.00 Tues–Sun (Oct–Apr) ⓝ HÉV: Aquincum ⓘ Admission charge

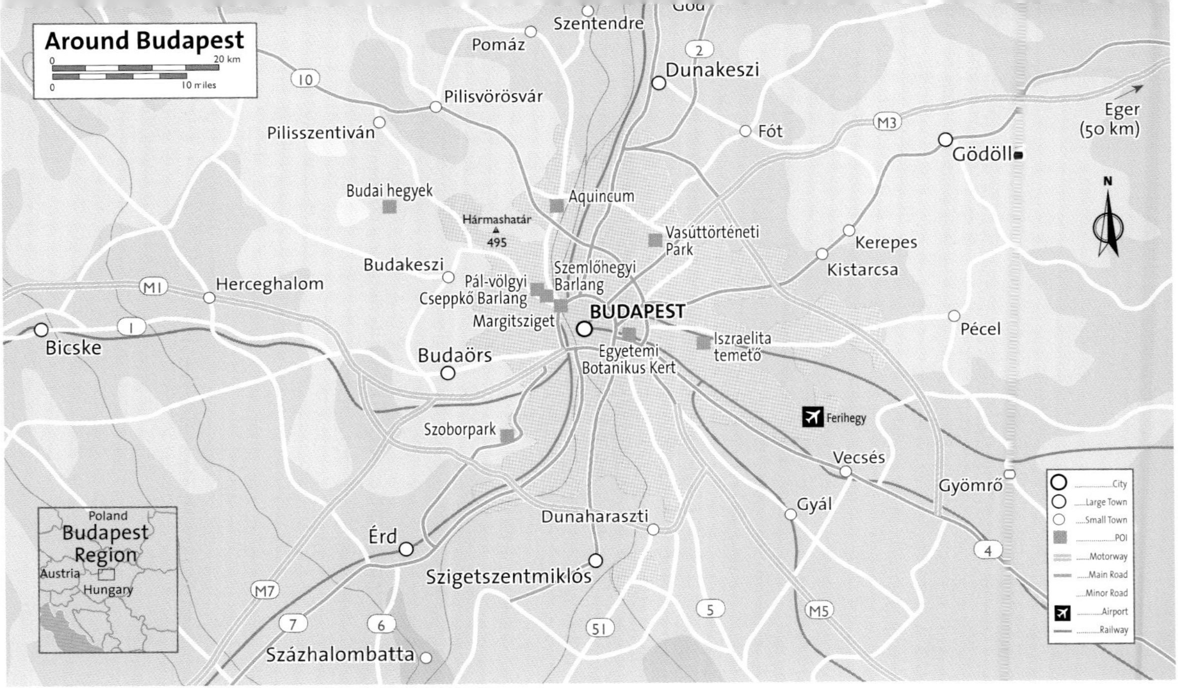
Around Budapest
0
20 km
0
10 miles
Szentendre
Pomáz
2
Dunakeszi
10
Pilisvörösvár
Pilisszentiván
Fót
M3
Eger
(50 km)
Gödöll
N
Budai hegyek
Aquincum
Hármashatár
495
Vasúttörténeti
Park
Kerepes
Kistarcsa
Budakeszi
M1
Herceghalom
Pál-völgyi
Cseppkő Barlang
Szemlőhegyi
Barlang
BUDAPEST
Margitsziget
Pécel
I
Bicske
Budaörs
Iszraelita
temető
Egyetemi
Botanikus Kert
Ferihegy
Szoborpark
Vecsés
Gyömrő
Gyál
Dunaharaszti
Érd
Szigetszentmiklós
Poland
Budapest
Region
Austria
Hungary
M7
7
6
51
5
M5
4
Százhalombatta
City
Large Town
Small Town
POI
Motorway
Main Road
Minor Road
Airport
Railway

Budai hegyek (Buda Hills)

Head for the hills (in particular, Széchenyi hegy, Sváb hegy, János hegy and Hármashatár hegy)! From Fasor tér, take the *fogaskerekű-vasút* (cogwheel railway) or the *libegő* (chairlift) up to the top. A mecca for nature lovers, the Buda Hills (at around 400–500 m, or 1,300–1,600 ft, above sea level) lie to the northwest of the city centre, and offer clean air and endless woods with well-marked tourist trails. In addition to walking and cycling, the most popular means of getting around is the **Children's Railway** (ⓦ www.gyermekvasut.com), a narrow-gauge railway that is operated by specially trained children.

The **Budakeszi Wildlife Park** (ⓣ (23) 451 783 ⓦ www.vadaspark-budakeszi.hu) occupies more than 300 hectares (750 acres) of woodland, where you can see real Budapest party animals (of the boar and wolf persuasion) roaming naturally. There's a walking safari tour that'll take you to all the best parts of the park, with a guide who will know what to do if you have a close encounter of the scary kind. Incorporate a visit to Erzsébet lookout tower. This tiny castle-like building, which was damaged when the giant red star was crudely strapped to its zenith, affords stunning views of Budapest. From here, you can get the chairlift back down to Buda.

Egyetemi Botanikus Kert (University Botanical Gardens)

Spread over 3 hectares (7 acres) of land, these peaceful gardens belong to the Eötvös Loránd University. An easy escape to where palms sway and children play – perfect for a picnic. ⓐ VIII. Illés utca 25 ⓣ (1) 314 0535 ⓛ 09.00–17.00 daily ⓣ Metro: Klinikák

Iszraelita temető (Jewish Cemetery)

Opened in 1893, the city's main Jewish cemetery is a long tram ride from the centre of town. More than 500,000 people are buried here,

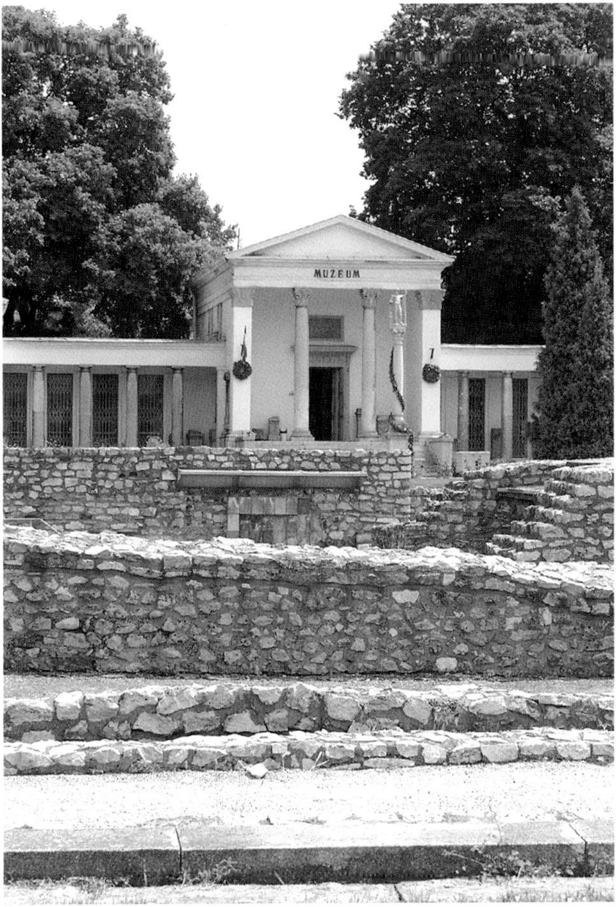

Aquincum – Roman ruins in the Budapest suburbs

Margaret Island is a quiet, green oasis

many in vast and elaborate tombs that bear witness to the wealth and influence afforded the Budapest Jews before World War II. Here you will find Hungary's most moving Holocaust memorial: a set of nine walls with the names of victims etched into it. Only about 7,000 names appear, 1 per cent of the estimated 700,000 Hungarian Jews who perished in the war. Survivors and relatives continue to pencil in hundreds of additional names. The cemetery is still in use today. ⓐ X. Kozma utca 6 ⓑ 08.00–16.00 Mon–Thur, 08.00–14.00 Fri & Sun ⓒ Metro: Blaha Lujza tér, then tram 37

Margitsziget (Margaret Island)

This island oasis in the heart of Budapest is neither Buda nor Pest, but Margaret Island. Inhabited since Roman times, it was named after Princess Margaret, daughter of the 13th-century King Béla IV. Poor nine-year-old Margaret didn't get a chance to enjoy the splendour of her island, as King Béla made a pact with God that he would give her to a nunnery built on the island in return for some heavenly protection against the Mongols. The ruins of the convent are still visible today on the island's east bank. Since then, medieval kings have gambolled about, monks have gone about their quiet business and Budapesters from the 1860s onwards have made the island their playground. If you're not into the peace and tranquillity, you can visit a UNESCO-protected water tower, a musical fountain, an open-air stage, the Palatinus Strand swimming pool, two spa hotels or various restaurants and cafés that dot the island. Pedal cars can be hired and picnicking is recommended. ⓒ Metro: Nyugati pu, then bus 26 or tram 4 or 6

Pál-völgyi Cseppkő Barlang (Pálvölgyi Stalactite Cave)

This cave is known for its interesting stalactite formations that resemble animals (some say elephants, some say crocodiles; whatever you say, some interesting psychological profiling is sure to follow). Much of the cave is accessible by public steps, but some of the more interesting formations need to be seen with a guide. The air is supposed to have a curative medicinal effect – it is said to be especially good for hangovers. Remember to bring a sweater because the caves are cool. ⓐ II. Szépvölgyi út 162 ⓣ (1) 325 9505 ⓦ www.barlangaszat.hu ◷ 10.00–16.00 Tues–Sun Ⓝ Bus: 65 ❶ Admission charge

Szemlőhegyi Barlang (Szemlő Hill Cave)

The forlorn entrance to the cave doesn't hint at the marvels you'll see once inside. The remarkable formations of pisolite, which look like bunches of grapes, were formed in areas where thermal water permeated the limestone. Its cool, moist air has a curative effect for those suffering from respiratory problems or an underactive sex drive. ⓐ II. Pusztaszeri út 35 ⓣ (1) 325 6001 ◷ 10.00–16.00 Wed–Mon Ⓝ Bus: 29 ❶ Admission charge

Szoborpark (Statue Park)

This park is either a kitsch gimmick or a commitment to remembering a harsh reality. While most of eastern Europe resolutely destroyed all socialist statuary after the fall of the Communist regime in 1989, Hungarians decided to preserve this history, plucking most of the public art in Budapest and surrounding areas and depositing it here, thus creating a bizarre theme park in tribute to some terrible times. It's not surprising, since Hungarians want to remember more than they want to forget. There is one exception: you won't find any Stalin here. After the 1956 Revolution, massive Stalin statues went missing. Back then, the various statues represented Soviet strength and unity.

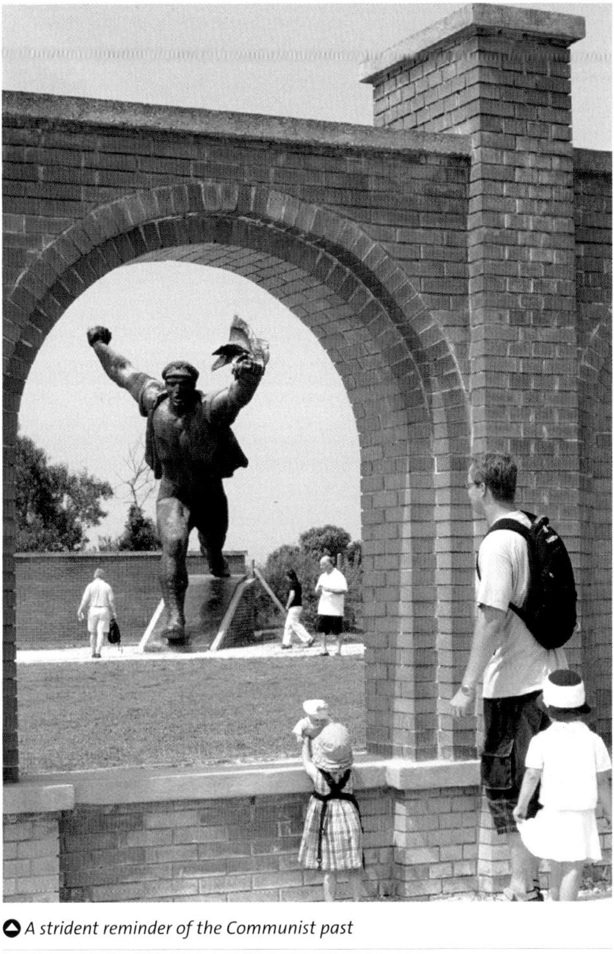

A strident reminder of the Communist past

Today, out on the edge of town, and placed in almost comical positions, they've lost much of their dignity. The collection is a bit on the sparse side. It's definitely worth a look, but not as impressive as most guidebooks would have you believe. The gift-shop sells all sorts of Communist-era memorabilia, such as T-shirts, medals and cassettes of Red Army marching songs. ⓐ XXII. Balatoni út ⓣ (1) 424 7500 ⓦ www.szoborpark.hu ⓘ 10.00–dusk daily ⓒ Bus: 150 ⓘ Admission charge

Vasúttörténeti Park (Railway History Park)

Remember the days you spent playing with a train set as a child? Those were the days! The Railway History Park is the place to pursue your childhood fantasy, and try your hand at being a conductor. There's plenty to gawk at: more than 100 old locomotives, including 50 vintage engines. Using a simulator modelled on the most powerful electric engine in Hungary, you can travel at 140 km (87 miles) per hour. Once you've practised, you'll have the chance to drive a real steam engine on a track 800 m (2,600 ft) long. If you get hungry with all the excitement, the Nostalgia Café serves light refreshments. From April to October, a vintage diesel shuttle train runs between Nyugati pu and the park. ⓐ XIV. Tatai út 95 ⓣ (1) 238 0558 ⓦ www.mavnosztaglia.hu ⓘ 10.00–18.00 Tues–Sun (Apr–Oct); 10.00–15.00 Tues–Sun (Nov, Dec & Mar); closed Jan & Feb ⓒ Bus: 30; HÉV: 14 ⓘ Admission charge

Wandering through the narrow streets of Eger

OUT OF TOWN
trips

Szentendre

Szentendre, a mere 20 km (12 miles) north of the hustle and bustle of Budapest, is a perfect day trip for those interested in escaping the heat of the capital and dipping their toes into Hungarian culture. During their brief stay, the Romans named the town Ulcisia Castra (Wolf Camp), then packed up and left. In the late 16th and early 17th centuries, Serbs fled to this area while escaping Ottoman attack, and settled here permanently, building wooden houses of worship, then later reaching deeper into their pockets to create the Baroque masterpieces we see today. Churches facing east on streets peppered with Serbian-style houses give Szentendre a distinctly Mediterranean feel.

Much of the Serbian population left in the 19th century, tired of fighting the flooding Danube and crop blight. As in so many small villages, disaster and lack of financial resources had a positive impact on preservation. The Industrial Revolution largely bypassed this cultural backwater by the Danube, leaving its lovely Baroque buildings intact.

In the 1920s, Hungarian artists rediscovered Szentendre. This town of seven spires gave them an artistic imperative to set up their easels, and a popular artists' colony was born. Tourists soon got wind of the creative atmosphere, making this the popular destination it is today. In a town with a population of 20,000, it's rare to see ancient churches, historical and contemporary museums, small galleries, chic cafés, affordable restaurants and hotels, and tacky souvenir shops all comfortably sharing the same space. Grand Baroque houses teeter on haphazardly built streets; unexpected alleyways lead just as often to a grandmother's kitchen as to an Orthodox church; and artists strive to capture

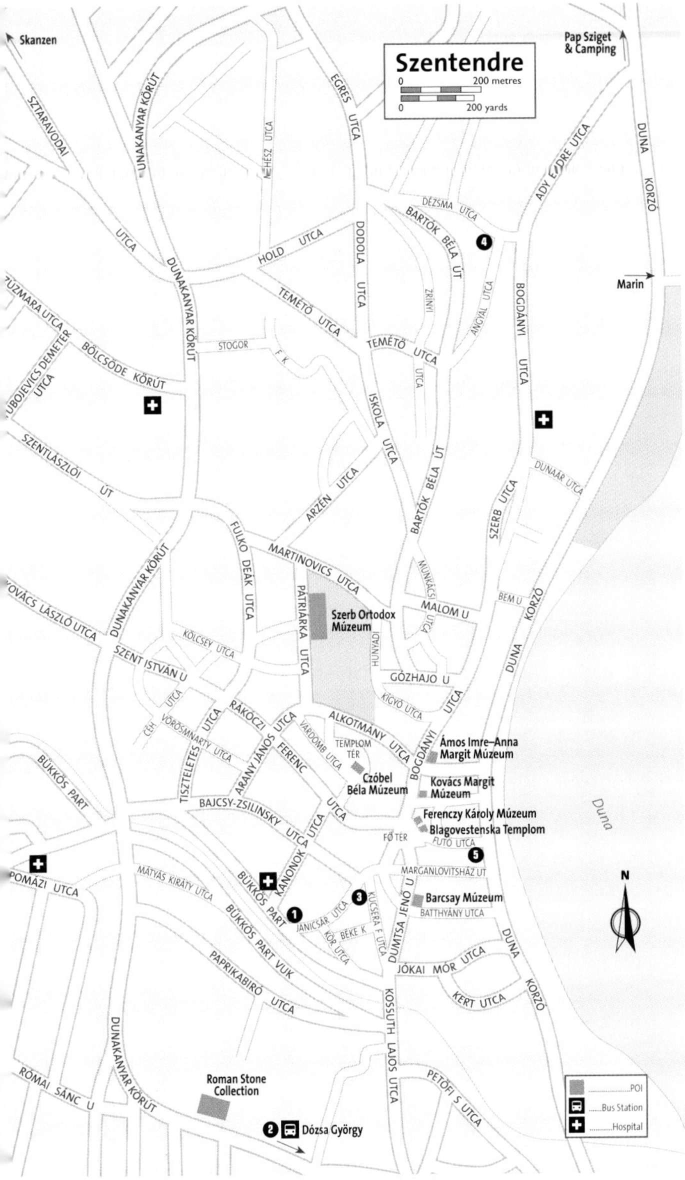
Szentendre
0 200 metres
0 200 yards
Skanzen
Pap Sziget & Camping
Marin
Szerb Ortodox Múzeum
Ámos Imre–Anna Margit Múzeum
Kovács Margit Múzeum
Czóbel Béla Múzeum
Ferenczy Károly Múzeum
Blagovestenska Templom
Barcsay Múzeum
Roman Stone Collection
Dózsa György
Duna
N
POI
Bus Station
Hospital
SZTARAVODAI UTCA
DUNAKANYAR KÖRÚT
EGRES UTCA
MÉHÉSZ UTCA
HOLD UTCA
DODOLA UTCA
DÉZSMA UTCA
BARTÓK BÉLA ÚT
ADY ENDRE UTCA
DUNA KORZÓ
TEMETŐ UTCA
ZRÍNYI
ANGYAL UTCA
BOGDÁNYI UTCA
PÚZMARA UTCA
LUBOJEVICS DEMETER UTCA
BÖLCSŐDE KÖRÚT
STOGOR
ISKOLA UTCA
SZENTLÁSZLÓI ÚT
DUNAÁR UTCA
ARZÉN UTCA
SZERB UTCA
FULKO DEÁK UTCA
MARTINOVICS UTCA
MUNKÁCSI UTCA
KOVÁCS LÁSZLÓ UTCA
PATRIÁRKA UTCA
MALOM U
BEM U
KÖLCSEY UTCA
HUNYADI
SZENT ISTVÁN U
GŐZHAJÓ U
KÍGYÓ UTCA
RÁKÓCZI UTCA
CÉH UTCA
VÖRÖSMARTY UTCA
TISZTELETES UTCA
ARANY JÁNOS UTCA
FERENC UTCA
VÁRDOMB UTCA
TEMPLOM TÉR
ALKOTMÁNY UTCA
BÜKKÖS PART
BAJCSY-ZSILINSZKY UTCA
FŐ TÉR
FUTÓ UTCA
MARGANLOVITSHÁZ UT
POMÁZI UTCA
MÁTYÁS KIRÁLY UTCA
KANONOK UTCA
JANICSÁR UTCA
KÖR UTCA
BÉKE K
KUCSERA F UTCA
DUMTSA JENŐ U
BATTHYÁNY UTCA
BÜKKÖS PART VUK
JÓKAI MÓR UTCA
KERT UTCA
PAPRIKABÍRÓ UTCA
KOSSUTH LAJOS UTCA
PETŐFI S UTCA
RÓMAI SÁNC U

the mottled hues of yesteryear. The Orthodox churches still function, breathing the air of the past into a town that hasn't forgotten its origins.

GETTING THERE

By rail

The HÉV suburban train will take you from Batthyány tér to Szentendre in just 45 minutes. Trains marked 'Szentendre' run every 20 minutes throughout the day, until 23.00. Buy your tickets at the station. For timetable information, call ⓣ (1) 368 8814 or see ⓦ www.bkv.hu

By road

Volánbusz buses go from Árpád híd bus station to Szentendre with varying frequency between 06.30 and 22.40 each day. They arrive at bay 5 of Szentendre bus station, right next to the HÉV terminus. The journey takes 30 minutes. Buy your tickets on the bus. For timetable information, call ⓣ (26) 382 0888 or see ⓦ www.volanbusz.hu

By water

This is the most recommended and romantic route, which follows the gently curving Danube from Budapest to Szentendre in a little over an hour-and-a-half. The boat leaves the Mahart quay at Vigadó tér each day at 10.30 and 14.30. A return boat leaves the quay at Szentendre at 17.00 and 19.00. Boats usually run until mid-October. Buy your tickets at the quayside, with round trips from Vigadó tér to Szentendre costing 2,235 HUF. For timetable information, call ⓣ (1) 318 1223 or see ⓦ www.mahartpassnave.hu

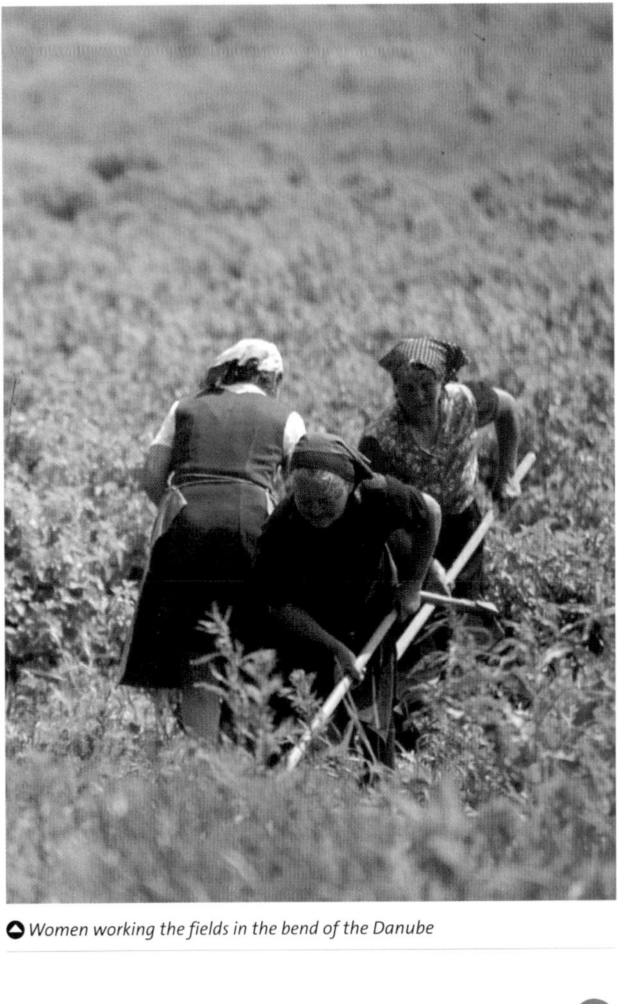

Women working the fields in the bend of the Danube

Szentendre's Blagovestenska Church

TOURIST INFORMATION

So many tourists, so many tourist information centres. The following are the most helpful:

IBUSZ Gives you all the information you need to make the most of your time in Szentendre. ⓐ Corner of Bogdányi út and Gőzhajó utca ⓣ (26) 310 181 ⓦ www.ibusz.hu ⓛ 09.00–17.00 Mon–Fri, 10.00–14.00 Sat & Sun (Apr–Oct); 09.00–16.00 Mon–Fri (Nov–Mar)

Jági Utazási Has very friendly and knowledgeable staff, who will be glad to help you with your itinerary and make fair and impartial recommendations for the best eats and sleeps in town. ⓐ Kucsera Ferenc utca 15 ⓣ (26) 500 252 ⓛ 10.00–18.00 Mon–Fri (in season); 09.00–17.00 Mon–Fri (out of season)

Tourinform Provides you with maps and an earful of information about concerts, exhibitions and accommodation across Szentendre. ⓐ Dumtsa Jenő utca 22 ⓣ (26) 317 965 ⓛ 09.00–19.00 Mon–Fri, 09.00–14.00 Sat & Sun (Apr–Oct); 09.00–17.00 Mon–Fri (Nov–Mar)

SIGHTS & ATTRACTIONS

Szentendre is centred on Fő tér, its main square, with windy, cobbled streets radiating in all directions. Be assured that you will have no problem locating art galleries, souvenir shops or cafés, which seem to sprout from every crooked street corner. In the middle of Fő tér stands the Memorial Cross, which was erected by townsfolk in gratitude for being spared from the plague, another plus in living far removed from the big city.

Ámos Imre–Anna Margit Múzeum

Once an artist couple's home, this museum shows how opposites attract. Margit Anna's work is surprisingly accessible, harking back to children's paintings and folk themes. Imre Ámos's art is haunting, relating back to his Jewish heritage, and some of his best work was done between periods of forced labour on the Russian front. His last work predicts his own demise; he died of typhus. ⓐ Bogdányi utca 12 ⓣ (26) 310 790 ◷ 10.00–18.00 daily ⓘ Admission charge

Barcsay Múzeum

Jenő Barcsay (1900–88) could be seen to epitomise Hungarian 20th-century art as a proponent of constructivism, an art movement of the 1920s that rejected 'pure' art forms and favoured socialist art. Through his public-building mosaics and wall textiles, we can see his creative genius at its best. The *Madman of the Village*, *Working Girl* and *Working Woman* are excellent examples of how he escaped the restrictions of socialism through expressionism. ⓐ Dumtsa Jenő utca 10 ⓣ (26) 310 244 ◷ 10.00–18.00 Tues–Sun ⓘ Admission charge

Blagovestenska Templom (Blagovestenska Church)

If you get the feeling you're being watched, that's perhaps because all of the icons in this church are in fact looking at you. This use of iconography was the most effective way to get the illiterate masses to pay attention during services. The rococo windows facing out on to Görög utca will also catch your eye. This Serbian Orthodox church dates from the mid-18th century. ⓐ Fő tér 4 ⓗ 10.00–17.00 Tues–Sun

Czóbel Béla Múzeum

This museum is housed in what was once a Catholic school on Szentendre's Castle Hill. Béla Czóbel (1883–1976) lived and worked from 1940 to 1966 in Szentendre, and from 1966 to 1967 in Budapest. The selection of works on display date from these periods and are mounted alongside information about both the artist and his paintings – helpfully provided in English. He's so popular that some of his art was lifted from the Museum of Fine Arts in Budapest (see page 94). ⓐ Templom tér 1 ⓣ (26) 312 721 ⓗ 10.00–18.00 Tues–Sun (mid-Mar–Sept); 13.00–17.00 Wed–Sun (Oct–mid-Mar) ⓘ Admission charge

Ferenczy Károly Múzeum

This museum contains historical, archaeological and ethnographic collections, as well as paintings, and is dedicated to the art of the extraordinary Ferenczy family, particularly the patriarch Károly Ferenczy, one of Hungary's most famous Impressionists and a member of the Nagybánya School. Works by Ferenczy's children, who were excellent artists in their own right, are also on display here. ⓐ Fő tér 6 ⓣ (26) 310 244 ⓗ 10.00–18.00 Tues–Sun (mid-Mar–Sept); closed Oct–mid-Mar ⓘ Admission charge

Kovács Margit Múzeum

Margit Kovács (1907–77) is a celebrated potter in Hungary. The museum limits entry to 20 people at a time, so try to visit either early in the morning or at lunchtime. ⓐ Vastagh György utca 1

(26) 310 244 10.00–18.00 Tues–Sun (mid-Mar–Sept); closed Oct–mid-Mar Admission charge

Pap Sziget (Priest's Island)

If you bring swimming gear to Szentendre, you can take a bus to this little island at the northern end of town, which boasts thermal waters in outdoor bathing pools. Facilities include some lockers in which to stash your cash, as well as towel hire. It's a 20-minute walk, or take the bus for Leányfalu and Visegrád; when you pass the bridge, get out at Pap Sziget.

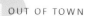

Skanzen

This open-air museum is 5 km (3 miles) from Szentendre. It's a living museum that faithfully depicts village life in Hungary from the end of the 18th century to the beginning of the 20th century. The villagers living under the thatched roofs of the village show visitors how to weave, cook, smith and work wood with all the historical tools of the trade. A market replete with farm animals milling about makes this a perfect excursion if you have children.

Skanzen re-creates Hungarian village life

ANOTHER MUSEUM, ANYONE?

If you're into twee museums, try the **Szabó Marzipan Museum** (ⓐ Dumtsa Jenő utca 14), which serves a marzipan version of Michael Jackson, or the **Dobos Confectionery Museum** (ⓐ Nosztalgia Ház, Bogdányi utca 2), where you can get some real Dobostorta (chocolate cake with a hard caramel topping). Or what about the **House of Folk Arts** (ⓐ Rákóczi utca 1) or the **Roman Stone Collection** (ⓐ Dunakanyari Boulevard 1), where you'll find ancient artefacts from the Roman town of Ulcisia Castra? The **Art Mill** (ⓐ Bogdányi utca 32) is a living workshop of contemporary arts with exhibitions. The **Baby Museum** (ⓐ Sas utca 18) is fun for children, as is the **National Wine Museum** (ⓐ Bogdányi utca 10) for harried parents and wine lovers.

To get there, take the bus from bay 7 of Szentendre's bus station. By car, follow route 11, and turn left at Sztaravodai utca. A family ticket is available, as well as English-language information about the museum. ⓣ (26) 502 500 ⓦ www.skanzen.hu ⓛ 09.00–17.00 Tues–Sun (Apr–Oct); 10.00–15.00 Sat & Sun (Nov); closed Dec–Mar ⓘ Admission charge

Szerb Ortodox Múzeum (Serbian Orthodox Museum)

This museum has a collection of icons from the 16th to 19th centuries, liturgical vessels and Ottoman-period scrolls in Arabic. Information is in English. ⓐ Pátriárka utca 5 ⓣ (26) 312 399 ⓛ 10.00–17.00 Tues–Sun (Apr–Oct); 10.00–16.00 Fri–Sun (Nov–Mar) ⓘ Admission charge

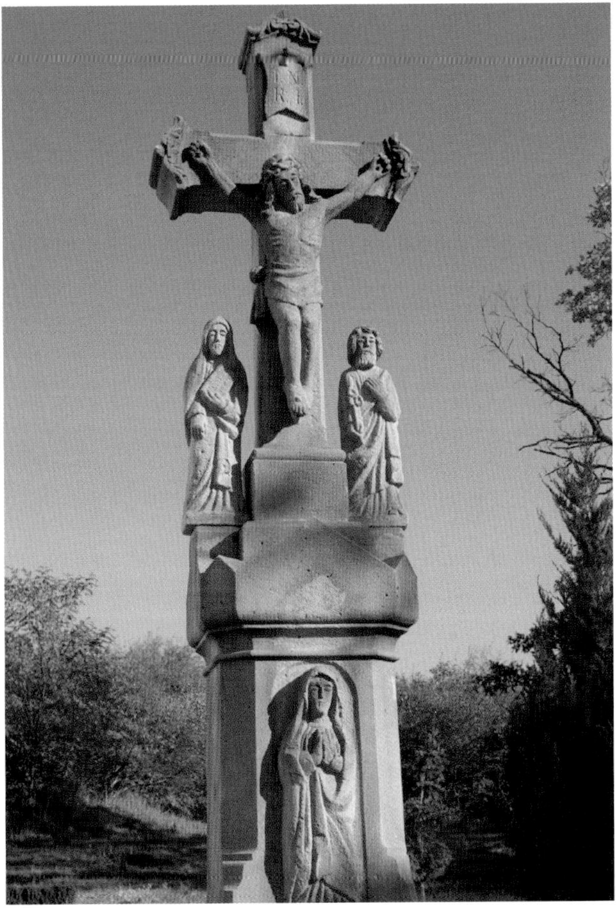

A stone cross with statues of Mary, the Apostles and Jesus at Skanzen

TAKING A BREAK

Cafés, restaurants and pubs spill out on to the pavements in the summer, giving the streets of Szentendre that European, lived-in look. With so many places to choose from, you will be hard-pressed to stay hungry. Most are concentrated around Fő tér and along the river. If you're interested in checking out the local music scene, there are a few music clubs in town.

Kedvenc Kifőzde £ ❶ A small lunch spot that serves some of the best quick meals in town. ⓐ Bükköspart 21 ⓣ (26) 319 186 ⓑ 12.00–16.00 Mon–Fri, 12.00–15.00 Sat

Mar Mediterraneo £ ❷ Warm and friendly, serving light salads and other dishes with a Mediterranean flair. ⓐ Pannónia utca 8 ⓣ (26) 314 185 ⓑ 12.00–22.00 daily

Rab Ráby £ ❸ A favourite with the locals, specialising in delicious fish dishes. ⓐ Kucsera Ferenc utca 1/a ⓣ (26) 310 819 ⓑ 12.00–22.00 Tues–Sun

Dézsma Étterem ££ ❹ Romantic, classy Hungarian eatery with three levels including a cool wine cellar and an extensive wine list. ⓐ Dézsma utca 2 ⓑ 12.00–22.00 Tues–Thur, 12.00–24.00 Fri & Sat, 12.00–21.00 Sun

Promenade Vendéglő ££ ❺ Gorgeous tavern along the Danube with terraces for summer days and a dining room and cosy wine cellar for chilly winters. Try the grilled lamb cutlets. ⓐ Futó utca 4 ⓣ (26) 312 626 ⓦ www.promenade-szentendre.hu ⓑ 12.00–22.00 daily

ACCOMMODATION

HOTELS & GUESTHOUSES

Centrum Panzió £ Big rooms, some with river views, and staff catering to your every need: massages, a play area for children with toys, and a filling breakfast. ⓐ Duna korzó, on the river north of Fő tér ⓣ (26) 302 500 ⓦ www.hotelcentrum.hu

Corner Panzió £ Set in a historical house, the rooms have been converted tastefully, with lots of blond wood and simple IKEA-like furnishings. A quiet family hotel in the heart of town. ⓐ Duna korzó 4 ⓣ (26) 301 524 ⓦ www.radoczy.hu

Hotel Róz £ A friendly guesthouse with a small garden overlooking the Danube for breakfast when weather permits. All rooms have 3-star amenities, and the hotel has its own restaurant serving fish, chicken and, of course, goulash. ⓐ Pannónia utca 6/b ⓣ (26) 310 979 ⓦ www.hotelrozszentendre.hu

Mathias Rex Panzió £–££ A wide range of rooms in this bed and breakfast, which also has a garden, secure parking, good breakfasts and a non-smoking floor. ⓐ Kossuth utca 16 ⓣ (26) 505 570 ⓦ www.mathiasrexhotel.hu

CAMPSITE

Pap Sziget (Priest's Island) £ Pap has a campsite for tents and caravans. You can also rent a bungalow. ⓣ (26) 310 697 ⓦ www.pap-sziget.hu ⓛ Apr–Oct, closed Nov–Mar

Eger

A minaret stands sentinel in this proud country town, 126 km (78 miles) northeast of Budapest, demarcating the furthest northern expansion in Europe of the Ottoman Turks. The siege of Eger lasted for over a month in 1552, when fewer than 2,500 soldiers and women repelled Turkish forces, who outnumbered them by 40 to 1, with whatever they could find – rocks, soup, hot fat, you name it. A proud moment in Hungarian history, the theme of 'The women defenders of Eger' is reflected in numerous paintings, poems and monuments throughout the country. Descendants of the famous women of Eger still meet today, but their activities in defence of the town are purely peaceful.

It's a town well worth defending. As Hungary's third most popular tourist destination, Eger offers an affordable taste of Hungary's history and cuisine, offering the truly Magyar experience for those who are interested. Its combination of soaring architectural sights, cosy wine cellars, a small-town feel and bustling, market-square activity is sure to please. The blend of old and new creates a lively atmosphere: upmarket shops, wine bars and restaurants, along with the ancient ruins of Eger Castle and the Turkish minaret, compete for your attention.

This historical wine area has been producing wines since the 11th century. Its best-known wine is Egri Bikavér, also known as Bull's Blood, forever linked with the strength and courage of Hungary's resistance to foreign powers. Don't leave Eger without testing some of the wonderful varieties in the nearby Szépasszony-völgy (Valley of Beautiful Women, see page 138), in the many old wine cellars dug into the hillside. The mould on many of the wine-cellar walls is so thick that you can stick a coin on it to commemorate your visit.

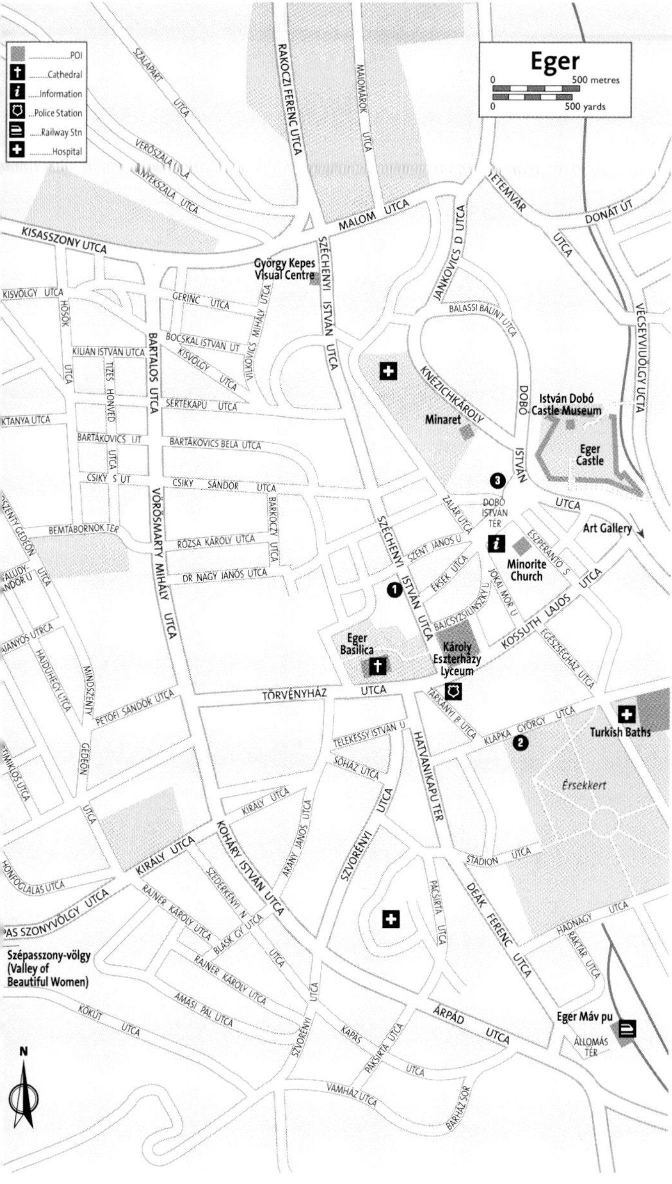
Eger
0
500 metres
0
500 yards
POI
Cathedral
Information
Police Station
Railway Stn
Hospital
N
György Kepes Visual Centre
István Dobó Castle Museum
Minaret
Eger Castle
Art Gallery
Minorite Church
Eger Basilica
Károly Eszterházy Lyceum
Turkish Baths
Érsekkert
Eger Máv pu
ÁLLOMÁS TÉR
DOBÓ ISTVÁN TÉR
Szépasszony-völgy (Valley of Beautiful Women)
KISASSZONY UTCA
MALOM UTCA
SZÉCHENYI ISTVÁN UTCA
RAKOCZI FERENC UTCA
MAJOMAROK UTCA
SZALAPART UTCA
VERŐSZALA UTCA
JANKOVICS D UTCA
DONÁT ÚT
VÉCSEYVIUÖLGY UCTA
BALASSI BALINT UTCA
KNÉZICHKÁROLY
DOBÓ ISTVÁN UTCA
GERINC UTCA
BOCSKAI ISTVÁN UT
KISVÖLGY UTCA
VILKOVICS MIHALY UTCA
KILIÁN ISTVÁN UTCA
TIZES HONVÉD
BARTALOS UTCA
SERTEKAPU UTCA
BARTÁKOVICS BELA UTCA
CSIKY SÁNDOR UTCA
BARKOCZY UTCA
VÖRÖSMARTY MIHÁLY UTCA
RÓZSA KÁROLY UTCA
DR NAGY JANOS UTCA
BEMTÁBORNOK TER
ZALAR UTCA
SZENT JANOS U
ÉRSEK UTCA
JÓKAI MOR U
BAJCSYZSILINSZKY U
ESZPERANTO S
KOSSUTH LAJOS UTCA
EGÉSZSÉGHÁZ UTCA
TÖRVÉNYHÁZ UTCA
TÁRKÁNYI B UTCA
KLAPKA GYÖRGY UTCA
TELEKESSY ISTVÁN U
SÓHÁZ UTCA
HATVANIKAPU TER
SZVORÉNYI UTCA
KIRÁLY UTCA
ARANY JANOS UTCA
KOHÁRY ISTVÁN UTCA
PETŐFI SANDOR UTCA
MINDSZENTY
HAJDÚHEGY UTCA
GEDEON
SZEDERKENYI N
RAJNER KÁROLY UTCA
BLASK GY UTCA
AMÁSI PAL UTCA
KŐKÚT UTCA
PAS SZONYVÖLGY UTCA
HONFOGLALÁS UTCA
PACSIRTA UTCA
STADION UTCA
DEÁK FERENC UTCA
HADNAGY UTCA
RAKTÁR UTCA
ÁRPÁD UTCA
KAPÁS
PAKSIRTA UTCA
VAMHÁZ UTCA
BARHÁZ SOR
KISVÖLGY UTCA
HŐSÖK UTCA
KTANYA UTCA
BARTÁKOVICS UT
CSIKY S UT
1
2
3

There are quite a few festivals and events happening in Eger during the summer, the cream of the crop being the Bull's Blood wine competition in July, and Eger Baroque Days from the end of July to mid-August, a splendiferous mix of classical concerts, dancing, laser light shows, theatre performances and cinema. Go to www.egeronline.com for more information about events.

GETTING THERE

By rail

From Budapest's Keleti Station, there are 34 trains leaving for Eger daily; the journey takes about two hours. The railway station in Eger is on Állomás tér, about one km (half a mile) from the town centre. Fares depend on the time of day you travel, so check before buying your ticket.

By road

Take the M3 motorway in the direction of Miskolc, then exit at Füzesabony and follow the signs to Eger. There are a few car parks in town and you can buy your parking ticket at the coin-operated machines nearby. The historical town centre is only open to pedestrians and drivers with permits.

SIGHTS & ATTRACTIONS

All of Eger's historical sites are within easy walking distance if you start at Dobó István tér, the main square of town. The **Minorite Church**, a fine 18th-century Baroque gem, is worth a look. Two statues dominate the square: one of István Dobó, town defender during the great siege, and the other of Magyars fighting against the Turks.

A view over Eger's rooftops

The István Dobó Castle Museum is one of the most popular in Hungary

TOURIST INFORMATION

For information, or securing accommodation, visit **Tourinform**.
ⓐ Bajcsy-Zsilinsky Endre utca 9 ⓣ (36) 517 715 ◷ 09.00–18.00 Mon–Fri, 15.00–17.00 Sat & Sun (in season); 09.00–17.00 Mon–Fri, 09.00–13.00 Sat, closed Sun (out of season)

The famous **Eger Castle** is a prominent stronghold visible from just about anywhere in town. You can wander the grounds free of charge, or visit the two museums that make their homes there. The **István Dobó Castle Museum** is choc-a-bloc with Turkish artefacts, and gives you the general history of the castle. **Eger Art Gallery** has a fine collection of Hungarian artists (◷ 10.00–17.00 Tues–Sun (summer); 10.00–16.00 Tues–Sun (winter) ⓘ Admission charge).

Just to the west of the castle, on Harangöntő utca, is Eger's imposing **minaret**, a visible reminder of the Turkish presence in the area. Though the town valiantly fought against the Ottoman Empire in 1552, it only stalled it for a few years. In 1596, Sultan Mohammed III was able to capture the castle, and the Turks ruled Eger until 1687, building mosques and baths. After the Turks retreated, there were only 3,500 residents in the town, including 600 Muslims who converted to Christianity and assimilated into Hungarian life. The minaret, which is 35 m (115 ft) tall, survives to this day in remarkably good condition, although the mosque that it belonged to was destroyed. For a small fee, you can ascend its cramped and dizzying spiral staircase and be rewarded with a spectacular view of the town below. Buy tickets for the minaret at its base (◷ 10.00–18.00 daily (summer); 10.00–16.00 daily (winter)).

South of the minaret on Eszterházy tér is the second-largest church in Hungary, Eger's **Basilica** (🕒 06.00–19.00 daily). This neoclassical building was built in the 1830s, replacing a medieval church that stood on the same spot. If you catch it in time to hear an organ recital in the summer, you'll bear witness to its awesome acoustics.

Opposite the basilica is the **Károly Eszterházy Lyceum** (🕒 09.30–15.00 Tues–Sun, closed Mon (summer); 09.30–13.00 Sat & Sun, closed Mon–Fri (winter)), Eger's finest example of 18th-century architecture. It's worth climbing up to the 11th storey and gazing out from the observatory at the top. Have a look at the frescoes that decorate the ceiling of the library. The latter contains the first Hungarian printed book, dating from 1473. Outdoor performances are frequently scheduled in the summer months.

Eger's **Turkish Baths** (ⓐ Fürdő utca 1–3 🕒 14.30–21.00 Mon–Fri, 09.00–21.00 Sat & Sun ⓦ www.egertermal.hu) were built at the start of the 17th century, and are perfect to soothe tired travel muscles. They're mixed-sex, with spa services posted in English.

The former home of Serbian fairy-tale author Mihály Vitkovics, now the **György Kepes Visual Centre** (ⓐ Széchenyi István út 55 ⓣ (36) 412 023), is worth a visit for an insight into local 18th-century literature.

TAKING A BREAK

There are cake shops and snack stands all around town where you can fuel up satisfyingly and cheaply. There aren't really any international eateries in this town, unless you consider pizza international. Here, it doesn't really matter where you go: you'll be served a surprisingly large platter of Hungarian specialities,

The Basilica in Eger is Hungary's second-largest church

Eger's restaurants serve hearty Hungarian food

described on the menu with choice phrases like 'The pleasures of the women of Eger' 'Foot of peasant' and 'Cow steps on István Dobó Square'.

Dobos Cukrászda £ ❶ A conveniently located little restaurant and coffee house that serves strong coffee and breakfast early, before the summer heat sets in, on Dobó István tér. ⓐ Széchenyi István utca 6 ⓣ (36) 413 335 ◷ 09.30–20.00 daily

Fehér Szarvas Vadásztanya £ ❷ A hunting inn, conveniently located south of Dobó István tér, which offers a full range of Hungarian wild-game specialities complemented by some good Hungarian vintage. More restaurant than café, this is popular with locals and tourists alike, so make a reservation if you can. ⓐ Klapka György utca 8 ⓣ (36) 411 129 ◷ 12.00–24.00 daily

Senátor Ház £ ❸ Locals seem to flock to this place. Eger is one of the few places in Hungary that serves strong Turkish coffee, a great way to start the morning, especially when coupled with a *túró süti*, a Hungarian pastry filled with curd cheese and raisins. ⓐ Dobó István tér 11 ⓣ (36) 411 711 ⓦ www.senatorhaz.hu ◷ 11.00–22.00 daily

ACCOMMODATION

HOTELS & GUESTHOUSES

Garten Vendégház £ A welcome respite for those wanting to get away from it all. The views from this guesthouse located in the hills overlooking Eger are beautiful, but even nicer is the price you pay for such a pretty spot. ⓐ Legányi utca 6 ⓣ (36) 420 371

VALLEY OF BEAUTIFUL WOMEN

If you take a 30-minute walk southwest from town, or a quick taxi ride, you will end up at the Szépasszony-völgy (Valley of Beautiful Women). Carved into the hillside, more than 200 wine cellars offer their own special vintage. If you're lucky, you'll go to a wine cellar that serves up live music with the wine; it can get quite lively after a few. Grab a quick snack from the stands serving nuts and crisps around the wine cellars, or a meal from one of the restaurants in the nearby village – good for cleansing your palate before the next tasting. The cellars open at noon and close early, most around 22.00.

Bacchus Panzió £–££ This tidy little bed and breakfast, situated between the Valley of Beautiful Women and the centre of Eger, serves up lots of charm. The rooms are nicely furnished, and there's a garden at the back. ⓐ Szépasszony-völgy utca 29 ⓣ (36) 428 950 ⓦ www.bacchuspanzio.hu

Hotel Korona ££ Clean and cosy 3- and 4-star rooms on a quiet residential street near Dobó István tér. Breakfast and wellness-sauna, whirlpool and swimming pool served up in style. There's even a 200-year-old wine cellar on the property, where you can taste some of Eger's finest. ⓐ Tündérpart 5 ⓣ (36) 310 287 ⓦ www.koronahotel.hu

Hotel Minaret ££ Next to the minaret, this hotel offers simple and tidy digs with breakfast. It's a great price for the downtown

Wine cellars are carved into the hillside just outside Eger

location, and the hotel's friendly management adds to its charm. ⓐ Knézich Károly utca 4 ⓣ (36) 410 233

Hotel Romantik ££ This family-oriented 3-star is located in the centre of Eger, about 50 m (55 yds) from Széchenyi utca, Eger's main pedestrian street. ⓐ Csíky S utca 26 ⓣ (36) 310 456 ⓦ www.romantikhotel.hu

Senátor Ház ££ Sitting right on Dobó István tér, the location and price can't be beaten, neither can the atmosphere of this small, friendly hotel. ⓐ Dobó István tér 11 ⓣ (36) 411 711 ⓦ www.senatorhaz.hu

CAMPSITES

Tulipán Kemping ££ This campsite is within stumbling distance of the Szépasszony-völgy wine cellars and has shower and restaurant facilities, and cabins and caravans for rent. The proprietors also own the affordable **Hotel Rubinia**, located next to the site. ⓐ Szépasszony-völgy 71 ⓣ (36) 410 580 ⓔ info@hotelrubinia.hu ⓛ Apr–Oct, closed Nov–Mar

Tramlines run along the Danube

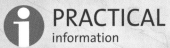

PRACTICAL information

Directory

GETTING THERE

By air

easyJet (ⓦ www.easyjet.com), **Jet2.com** (ⓦ www.jet2.com), **Wizz Air** (ⓦ www.wizzair.com), **BA** (ⓦ www.britishairways.com) and **Lufthansa** (ⓦ www.lufthansa.com) all fly to Budapest's Ferihegy Airport (see page 48), which is 24 km (15 miles) southeast of the city centre. It has three terminals: Terminal 1, which serves a small number of budget airlines; Terminal 2A, which serves **Malév Hungarian Airlines** (ⓦ www.malev.com); and the busy Terminal 2B, which serves most of the international and budget airlines and welcomes around four million passengers a year. For general information about the airport, call ⓣ (1) 296 9696; for flight information, call ⓣ (1) 296 5959 or visit ⓦ www.bud.hu. The journey time from UK airports is approximately two-and-a-quarter hours.

From North America, Alitalia and British Airways both fly routes into Budapest, with the flight time around nine hours from New York and 12 hours from Atlanta. Virgin Atlantic flies into Budapest, with a stopover in the UK, and the journey time is around 27 hours. If you're flying from New Zealand, you can book flights with BA or **Qantas** (ⓦ www.qantas.com.au), but again there are stopovers (the US/UK and Australia/Thailand, respectively), with the journey time around 29 hours. That's a lot of in-flight movies to watch...

Many people are aware that air travel emits CO_2, which contributes to climate change. You may be interested in the possibility of lessening the environmental impact of your flight through the charity **Climate Care** (ⓦ www.jpmorganclimatecare.com), which offsets your CO_2 by funding environmental projects around the world.

The Tisza Express to Moscow waits at Keleti Station

By rail

More than 50 trains a day provide direct links between Budapest and no fewer than 25 other capital cities. The city has three international railway stations – Keleti, Nyugati and Déli – all of which have a metro station. Trains from Vienna to Budapest run regularly, and the journey takes about three-and-a-half hours. For planning a longer train journey to Budapest, consult the monthly **Thomas Cook European Rail Timetable**, which has up-to-date schedules for European international and national train services (www.thomascookpublishing.com).

By road

International coach services run to and from **Népliget** coach station (ⓐ IX. Üllői út 131 ⓣ (1) 219 8063 ⓛ 04.30–23.00 daily). For planning a coach journey to Budapest, contact **Eurolines** (ⓦ www.eurolines.co.uk).

If you choose to drive yourself, be aware that speed limits are 130 km/h (80 mph) on motorways, 110 km/h (68 mph) on dual carriageways, 90 km/h (56 mph) on other roads and 50 km/h (31 mph) in built-up areas. It is compulsory to wear seat belts in both front and back seats and prohibited to use mobile phones when the car is in motion. There is zero tolerance of drink-driving in Hungary.

The M0 ring road and the M1, M3, M5 and M7 toll motorways will link you to Budapest from all directions, and you must pay the appropriate toll either at the border or at one of the larger petrol stations. Make sure you display the sticker in your windscreen.

The border crossings from Austria and Slovakia are hassle-free. Hungary no longer requires the international driving permit. Cars entering Hungary are required to have a sticker indicating the country of registration, a first-aid kit and an emergency warning triangle.

The Hungarian Automobile Club (ⓐ II. Rómer Flóris utca 8 ⓣ (1) 345 1800 ⓦ www.autoklub.hu) offers 24-hour roadside assistance and emergency roadside help (ⓣ 188 in a crisis).

By water

A hydrofoil service along the Danube runs from April to October. The journey to Budapest takes six-and-a-half hours from Vienna and four-and-a-half hours from Bratislava. You will arrive at Belgrad rakpart. The service is operated by **Mahart PassNave Ltd** (ⓣ (1) 484 4010 ⓦ www.mahartpassnave.hu).

ENTRY FORMALITIES

Citizens of the UK, the Republic of Ireland, the US, Canada, Australia, New Zealand and most countries in continental Europe need only a valid passport to enter Hungary for up to 90 days. Citizens of other countries should contact their Hungarian embassy for details of visa requirements or see www.mfa.gov.hu

Visitors to Hungary from within the EU are entitled to bring their personal effects and goods for personal consumption and not for resale, which can be up to 800 cigarettes and 10 litres of spirits. Those entering the country from outside the EU may bring 200 cigarettes (50 cigars, 250 g tobacco), 2 litres of wine and 1 litre of spirits. No meat or milk products are permitted to be brought into the country from inside or outside the EU.

MONEY

The Hungarian currency is the *forint* (HUF). Coins in circulation are 1, 2, 5, 10, 20, 50 and 100 HUF. Banknotes come in denominations of 200, 500, 1,000, 2,000, 5,000, 10,000 and 20,000 HUF. You can use your credit card in tourist-related businesses such as hotels, restaurants, petrol stations and the more central shops, but often not in museums, supermarkets and train or bus stations. For this reason, it's a good idea always to have some cash on you. ATMs are on just about every street corner and are the place to go for a quick top-up of finances. Euros, US dollars and British pounds are acceptable forms of payment at higher-end accommodation facilities.

If you want to change some money, there are convenient 24-hour exchange machines that offer good bank rates. You can find them in many places, such as Margit körút 43–45, Károly körút 20, Váci utca 40, Andrássy út 49 and elsewhere. Don't use Interchange or the exchange kiosks around Váci utca: they're a misleading rip-off, since they post

Police zip through the smaller streets of Budapest in their Smart cars

good rates that apply only if you change a lot of money. Don't even think about changing money on the black market; it's illegal, and you get better rates at the 24-hour exchange machines anyway.

HEALTH, SAFETY & CRIME

No jabs or inoculations are required for entry to Hungary. To be on the safe side, bring enough of any prescription or other medication you may need. Always pack a copy of all prescriptions in case you run out of any medication. You can find sunscreen and other toiletries, in addition to over-the-counter medications, at any chemist. The biggest complaint among travellers is an upset stomach, probably brought on by mixing paprika and alcohol.

Air pollution in Budapest, though bad, is getting better, as the ring road now redirects long-distance lorries around the city. The water is perfectly safe to drink. Smoking is prohibited in all public places, including on public transport. Unfortunately for non-smokers, smoking is still publicly accepted in restaurants and pubs, so expect your lungs to get a little black in exchange for some ambience.

Budapest is generally a safe city, and violent street crime is practically non-existent. Boisterous drunks are a nuisance, but rarely pose a serious threat. That said, you should always be on the lookout for pickpockets, especially on crowded buses, trains and trams. Pickpockets generally work in teams, with one or more creating a distraction (bumping into people, falling down, staging a fake argument and so on), while a partner takes advantage. One way to protect yourself is by always carrying valuables in an inside pocket or in a money belt.

Be wary of overly friendly women, particularly on touristy thoroughfares. The *konzum lány*, or 'consumption girl', is an attractive young woman who approaches a foreigner, strikes up a conversation and then brings him to a bar she 'just happens to know'. After she gets him to buy her a drink, the foreigner is presented with an outlandish bill. A few brutes materialise out of nowhere and make the foreigner pay, and the girl goes back out on the street, ready for her next victim.

To register a complaint about a scam of any kind, contact the **Fogyasztóvédelmi Főfelügyelőség**, or **Bureau of Consumer Affairs** (ⓐ VIII. József körút 6 ⓣ (1) 459 4800 or 459 4945 ⓛ 08.00–18.00 Mon–Thur, 09.00–14.00 Fri).

OPENING HOURS

Banks 08.00–15.00 Mon–Thur, 08.00–13.00 Fri
Clothes shops 10.00–18.00 Mon–Sat
Food shops 07.00–18.00 Mon–Sat
Offices 08.00–16.00 Mon–Fri
Post Offices 08.00–16.00 Mon–Fri, 08.00–13.00 Sat

TOILETS

Few public toilets exist in Buda or Pest, so locals and tourists use the toilets in cafés and restaurants. You just have to pay the attendant after using the facilities. Toilets in shopping centres also provide quick relief.

Toilets in bars and wine or beer cellars are often free. Note also that while Budapest's main railway stations have public toilets, most metro stations do not.

Toilets signposted in Hungarian usually have the words *Nők* or *Női* (women) and *Férfiak* or *Férfi* (men). Occasionally, signs for *Hölgyek* (ladies) and *Urak* (gentlemen) also appear.

CHILDREN

You and your children will have an absolute blast in Budapest. The three main areas to go are the Buda Hills (see page 106), Margaret Island (see page 109) and the Városliget, or City Park (see page 93).

In the Buda Hills, you can go for long or short hikes, taking advantage of the fun modes of transport, such as the chairlift and special railways. On Margaret Island, the playground for adults and children in Budapest, you can hire a pedal car; visit a musical fountain, an old ruin and a small zoo (XIV. Városliget, Állatkerti körút 6–12 (1) 273 4900 www.zoobudapest.com), where children can pet some of the animals; or go splashing in the

Palatinus Strand (ⓐ XIII. Margitsziget ⓣ (1) 340 4505), a fantastic outdoor swimming pool, or Hajós Alfréd pool for more serious swimmers. In the Városliget, you can visit the **Fun Fair** (ⓐ XIV. Városliget, Állatkerti körút 14–16) or the **Capital Circus** (ⓐ XIV. Városliget, Állatkerti körút 7 ⓣ (1) 343 9630 ⓦ www.maciva.hu).

Elsewhere in the city, older children might enjoy the **Görzenál Skate and Leisure Park** (ⓐ III. Árpád fejedelem út 2000 ⓣ (1) 250 4800

Take the kids along to the zoo for a great day out

w www.gorzenal.hu). Meanwhile, the **Laser Theatre Planetarium** (a X. Népliget t (1) 265 0725 w www.lasertheatre.hu) has various musical programmes and educational shows. Science buffs will appreciate the **Palace of Wonders** (a II. Fény u. 20–22 t (1) 350 6131 w www.csodakpalotaja.hu), where they can get hands-on with science experiments. Buda Castle Labyrinth (see page 67) is great for entertaining kids of all ages.

COMMUNICATIONS

Internet

In Budapest, there's Internet access at just about every turn. Major hotels and shopping centres offer Internet facilities as well. To find wireless hotspots in Budapest, go to w www.hotspotter.hu

Phone

Hungary's modernised communications provider is Magyar Telekom. The quality of both landline and mobile services is good, with mobile services provided by T-Mobile, Vodafone and Pannon GSM.

For payphones, buy a phonecard at post offices, MOL petrol stations, travel agencies, Tesco supermarkets, newspaper kiosks, railway stations and T-Pont shops, for values of 800 HUF upwards. Coins (10, 20, 50 and 100 HUF) can also be used.

For directory enquiries dial t 198 and for international directory enquiries dial t 199.

Post

You can find square red postboxes with the post horn and envelope symbols throughout Budapest. Postage stamps are widely available at tobacconists.

TELEPHONING HUNGARY

To telephone Hungary from abroad, dial the international access code (00), followed by the country code (36), the appropriate area code (1 for Budapest, 36 for Eger, 26 for Szentendre) and finally the six- or seven-digit telephone number.

To make a long-distance call within Hungary, such as from Budapest to Szentendre, dial 06, followed by the area code (26) and the six-digit telephone number.

Mobile providers supply numbers beginning with 20, 30 or 70, followed by a regular seven-digit number.

TELEPHONING ABROAD

To telephone home from Hungary, dial the international access code (00), followed by the appropriate country code (61 for Australia, 1 for Canada or the US, 64 for New Zealand, 353 for the Republic of Ireland, 44 for the UK etc), the area code (minus the initial 0, in the case of the UK) and then the number you require.

The **Magyar Posta main post office** is at ⓐ V. Városház utca 18 ⓣ (1) 485 9041 ⓑ 08.00–20.00 Mon–Fri, 08.00–14.00 Sat ⓜ Metro: Deák Ferenc tér

There are also post offices near Keleti and Nyugati railway stations. The post office near Keleti is at ⓐ VIII. Baross tér 11/c ⓣ (1) 322 9013 ⓑ 07.00–21.00 Mon–Fri, 08.00–14.00 Sat. The post office near Nyugati is at ⓐ VI. Teréz körút 51–53 ⓣ (1) 353 0860 ⓑ 08.00–20.00 Mon–Fri, 08.00–14.00 Sat

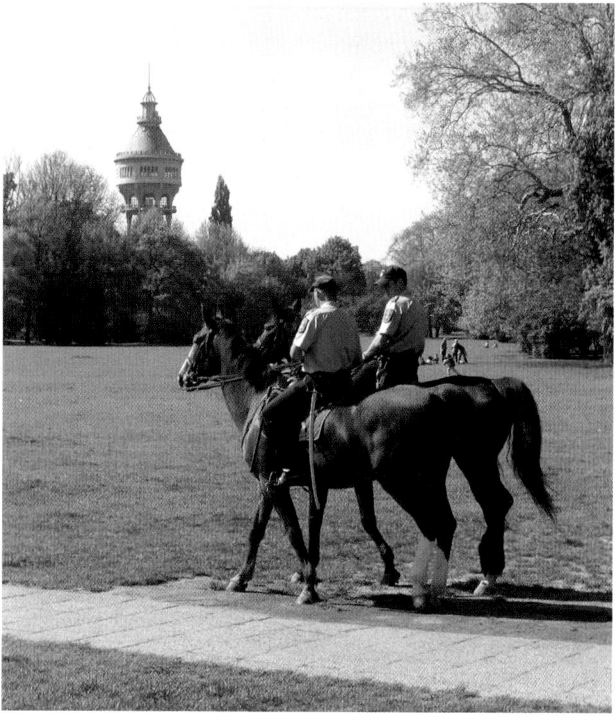

Mounted police on Margaret Island

ELECTRICITY

The electrical current is supplied at 220 volts. Standard continental two-pin plugs are used, so an adaptor will be required for British and non-continental appliances. Americans and Canadians with 110-volt appliances will also need a voltage transformer.

TRAVELLERS WITH DISABILITIES

Many Budapest buildings are inaccessible to disabled travellers, and public transport can be difficult. The good news is that EU norms have influenced policy, making Hungary's museums, newer buildings and some public transport accessible. Gellért Baths (see page 67), for instance, were renovated in 2007 to improve access. The yellow metro line has a special motorised chair at the Deák tér, Mexikói út and Széchenyi fürdő stops. For more information contact the **Hungarian Disabled Association (MEOSZ)** (ⓐ III. San Marco utca 76 ⓣ (1) 388 5529 or 388 2387 ⓦ www.meosz.hu ⓗ 08.00–17.00 Mon–Fri).

TOURIST INFORMATION

Tourinform Belváros ⓐ V. Sütő utca 2 ⓣ (1) 438 8080
ⓗ 08.00–20.00 daily
Tourinform Buda Castle ⓐ I. Szentháromság tér ⓣ (1) 488 0475
ⓗ 09.00–20.00 daily
Tourinform Oktogon ⓐ VI. Liszt Ferenc tér 11 ⓣ (1) 322 4098
ⓗ 10.00–18.00 Mon–Fri, 10.00–16.00 Sat & Sun

See also ⓦ www.budapestinfo.hu for more information.

BACKGROUND READING

Culture Shock! Hungary by Zsuzsanna Ardó. Offers an unflinching but affectionate insight into the character of a nation.
The Hungarians: A Thousand Years of Victory in Defeat by Paul Lendvai. An accessible, in-depth history of a proud, passionate people.
Living in Hungary by Jean-Luc Soulé and Alain Fleischer. Couples world-class photography with inspirational travel ideas, to make an up-close-and-personal guide to the Hungarian way of living.

Emergencies

The international emergency number is 112 and numbers for individual services are as follows:

Ambulance 104

Doctor (1) 311 1666

Fire 105

Police 107

To report a crime (in English) dial (1) 438 8080 or 06 80 555 111

MEDICAL SERVICES

For EU citizens, emergency medical treatment is provided free of charge in Hungary. The following are centrally located emergency chemists:

Mária XIII. Béke tér 11 (1) 320 8006

Óbuda III. Vörösvári út 84 (1) 368 6430

The following are surgeries with English-speaking doctors:

Belgyógyászati Klinika VIII. Korányi Sándor utca 2/a (1) 210 0278 By appointment Mon–Fri

Dr Rose Medical Center V. Roosevelt tér 7–8 (1) 377 6737 (non-stop hotline) 08.00–20.00 Mon–Fri

FirstMed Centers I. Hattyú utca 14, 5th floor (1) 224 9090 www.firstmedcenters.com 24 hrs

Rózsakert Medical Center II. Gábor Áron utca 74–78/a, 3rd floor (1) 392 0505 www.medical-center.hu 24 hrs

The following are surgeries with English-speaking dentists:

SOS Dent VI. Király utca 14 (1) 269 6010 24 hrs

Szent Rókus Kórház és Intézményei VIII. Gyulai Pál utca 2 (1) 266 8000

POLICE

If you are robbed, it's best to report it to the crime hotline (t (1) 438 8080, 06 80 201 303 or 107). If you need to fill in any forms, go to the **Central Police Station** (a XIII. Teve utca 4–6 t (1) 443 5500 Metro: Arpád híd).

EMBASSIES & CONSULATES

Australia a XII. Királyhágó tér 8–9 t (1) 457 9777 w www.ausembbp.hu
Canada a II. Ganz utca 12–14 t (1) 392 3360 w www.dfait-maeci.gc.ca/budapest
Ireland a V. Szabadság tér 7 t (1) 301 4960 w www.embassyofireland.hu
New Zealand does not have an embassy in Budapest, but contact either the British embassy or the honorary consulate t (1) 302 2484
South Africa a II. Gárdonyi Géza útca 17 t (1) 392 0999
UK a V. Harmincad utca 6 t (1) 266 2888 w www.britishembassy.hu
US a V. Szabadság tér 12 t (1) 475 4400 w www.usembassy.hu

EMERGENCY PHRASES

Help!	**Fire!**	**Stop!**
Segítség!	Tűz!	Állj!
Sheh-geet-shayg!	*Teewz!*	*Ahlly!*

Call an ambulance/a doctor/the police/the fire brigade!
Hivja a mentőket/orvost/rendőrséget/tűzoltókat!
Heev-yo o mehn-tur-keht/ohr-vohsht/rehn-dur-shay-geht/teewz-ohl-tooh-kot!

ACKNOWLEDGEMENTS
The publishers would like to thank the following individuals and organisations for supplying their copyright photographs for this book: Aquincum Museum, page 107; John Butterfield/iStockphoto.com, page 125; City Hotel Pilvax, page 37; Dreamstime.com (Belizar, page 131; Andrey Gatash, page 113; Peter Gustafson, page 33; Harryfn, page 7; Udvarházi Irén, pages 122–3; Jakatics, page 118; Krzysztof Kordys, page 135; Soundsnaps, page 146; Tomispin, page 27; Attila Vörös, page 143); Beata Laki, page 71; Klara Low, page 5; Gerrit Prenger, page 64; Claudio Recalcati, page 49; Shutterstock.com (Szabi, page 38; Yarchyk, page 75); SXC.hu (Orsolya Ganzler, page 152; Korosy Istvan, page 22; Attila Iván, page 45; Irina Reberšak, page 24); sziget2005.com, page 13; Tourism Office of Budapest, pages 9 & 149; Kádár Viktor, page 141; Wendy Wrangham, pages 19, 40–41, 59, 85 & 99; www.inpixtourism.com (an inpix.co.uk company), page 132; Helena Zukowski, page 117; The Hungarian National Tourist Office, all others.

Project editor: Kate Taylor
Copy editor: Paul Hines
Layout: Paul Queripel
Proofreaders: Cath Senker & Jan McCann

Send your thoughts to
books@thomascook.com

- **Found a great bar, club, shop or must-see sight that we don't feature?**
- **Like to tip us off about any information that needs a little updating?**
- **Want to tell us what you love about this handy little guidebook and more importantly how we can make it even handier?**

Then here's your chance to tell all! Send us ideas, discoveries and recommendations today and then look out for your valuable input in the next edition of this title.

Email the above address (stating the title) or write to:
pocket guides Series Editor, Thomas Cook Publishing, PO Box 227, Coningsby Road, Peterborough PE3 8SB, UK.

WHAT'S IN YOUR GUIDEBOOK?

Independent authors Impartial up-to-date information from our travel experts who meticulously source local knowledge.

Experience Thomas Cook's 165 years in the travel industry and guidebook publishing enriches every word with expertise you can trust.

Travel know-how Thomas Cook has thousands of staff working around the globe, all living and breathing travel.

Editors Travel-publishing professionals, pulling everything together to craft a perfect blend of words, pictures, maps and design.

You, the traveller We deliver a practical, no-nonsense approach to information, geared to how you really use it.

Useful phrases

English	Hungarian	*Approx pronunciation*
	BASICS	
Yes	Igen	*Ee-gehn*
No	Nem	*Nehm*
Please	Kérem	*Kay-rehm*
Thank you	Köszönöm	*Kuh-suh-nuhm*
Hello	Szervusz	*Sehr-voos*
Goodbye	Viszontlátásra	*Vee-sohnt-lah-tahsh-ro*
Excuse me	Elnézést	*Ehl-nay-zaysht*
Sorry	Bocsánat	*Bo-chah-not*
That's okay	Rendben van	*Rhend-ben von*
Do you speak English?	Beszél angolul?	*Beh-sayl on-goh-lool?*
Good morning	Jó reggelt	*Joh rehg-gehlt*
Good afternoon	Jó napot	*Joh no-poht*
Good evening	Jó estét	*Joh ehsh-tayt*
Goodnight	Jó éjszakát kívánok	*Joh ahy-so-kaht kee-vah-nohk*
My name is ...	A nevem ...	*O neh-vehm ...*
	NUMBERS	
One	Egy	*Ehdj*
Two	Kettő	*Kayt-tur*
Three	Három	*Hah-rohm*
Four	Négy	*Naydj*
Five	Öt	*Uht*
Six	Hat	*Hot*
Seven	Hét	*Hayt*
Eight	Nyolc	*Njohlts*
Nine	Kilenc	*Kee-lehnts*
Ten	Tíz	*Teez*
Twenty	Húsz	*Hoos*
Fifty	Ötven	*Urt-vehn*
One hundred	Száz	*Sahz*
	SIGNS & NOTICES	
Airport	Repülőtér	*Reh-pew-lur-tayr*
Railway station	Vasútállomás	*Vah-shooht-ahl-loh-mahsh*
Smoking/ No smoking	Dohányzóknak/ Nem dohányzóknak	*Doh-hahnj-zohk-nok/ Nehm doh-hahnj-zohk-nok*
Toilets	WC	*Vay-tsay*
Ladies/Gentlemen	Női/Férfi	*Nyr-ee/Fayr-fee*